Attention Late Bloomers: You're Right On Time!

Proven principles, interesting theories, practical tools, inspiring stories ... and some funny stuff, too, to help "late bloomers" of all ages achieve their hopes, wishes and dreams.

***

For additional copies:

The Posner Group
P.O. Box 244
West Stockbridge, MA 01266
posgroup@aol.com
www.jerryposner.com

***

Cover design by Robin O'Herin

JERRY D. POSNER

ATTENTION LATE BLOOMERS: YOU'RE RIGHT ON TIME!

2006

Attention Late Bloomers: You're Right
On Time!

TABLE OF CONTENTS

FOREWORD

I wanted to write a book that was fun to read, interesting, and truly helpful ... in that order.

DEDICATIONS,
ACKNOWLEDGMENTS,
THANK YOU NOTES,
AND LOVE LETTERS.

The "butterfly effect" is activated by every relationship and encounter.

This book is dedicated to my mother, Irene Rose Gurland Posner, who gets all of my jokes, even the little sneaky ones.

Thanks for the DNA.

Thanks for buying me that astrology book when I was 5.

Thanks SO much for waking me up to see Frank Zappa on the Dick Cavett show.

And, of course, the brisket.

And to my father Hyman L. Posner, a.k.a. George LaRue and Georgie Lakes ("the golfing comedian from F.L.A."), who taught me about finance, customer service and networking. He demonstrated "unconditional kindness" in business relationships and is still remembered as the "king" of Lyndhurst, NJ. Thanks for your DNA, too.

I am glad that Irene and George met, and liked each other enough (and long enough) to create me. When I'd gotten into hot water, they bailed me out. Thanks!

And ...

To Susan Jane Posner Russell, my excellent sister, her husband Rick and my niece Alison: I really did luck out in the sibling/in-law/niece department. I luv you guys!

Much gratitude to:

Don and Jackie Wescott, and Joan Zuckerman. Jackie, Don and I met in 1976, at PSI recording studios in Boston. Don impressed me with his talent, humor and kindness. I moved to the Berkshires from Southern California in 1989, partnering with Don and Jackie to publish *The Positive Times Journal* in the early to mid 1990s. Jackie's humor, wisdom and creative concepts are evident throughout this book, including the title concept "Attention Late Bloomers ... You're Right on Time." She is the most committed (and militant) optimist I know; an enthusiastic teacher of positivity, and a crackerjack astrologer.

I met Joan Zuckerman at Thomas Jefferson Jr. High School (Teaneck, NJ – late sixties). To this day, we talk on the phone for hours, just like we did back then. Joan is a compassionate, intuitive friend, who gives me valuable feedback and reality checks.

Karen Davis (special editorial assistance), Annie Herbert Emprima, Vicky Singer, and Joanne Spies—great friends, great pals, great people.

To Dave and John Pelletier, plus the staff and management of Tio Juan's Margaritas Restaurants, thanks for your support of my work, your kindness, enthusiasm, and friendship. You've helped my workshops and seminars bloom and blossom. Ditto to John Mathers, Scott Schiff, Kathy Hazelett. Thanks Canyon Ranch, Lenox MA., Greylock Federal Credit Union, Brunswick Corp., O'Connell Oil Associates, the managers of Crowne Plaza Hotel Pittsfield/Berkshires (Tom Guido, Don Bruce, Vince Barba, Nick Boulas, Renee Lepel, and Chuck Brush), my many clients, vendors and business friends.

Thanks to Gary Weiner, Mike Sussman, John Colbert, Bruce Weber, Dave Salzman, Mark Faulkner, John Bachman, Joanne Greene, Ellen Sachs, Barbara Peck, Bob Geary, Eliot Lane, Evie Bystrom-Herrera, Danny Robles, Jayne Church, Pamela Knisley, Beverly Banov Brown, and Beverly Dubiski.

Thank you Rosemary Nostas (T.J.J.H.S.), Barbara Wagner (T.H.S.), Bob and Myra Manning (The Book Pub), Barbara Rogers (Ramapo College), Ruth Ziering and Mama Mitchell (Emerson College), Vinny Parla (P.S.I.), E.C.P. and the chelas, Bob Zidel (KMDY), Steve Rubinstein (C.V.C.C.), Ron Straile (500 Marketing Group) Phil Weiner (WUPE/WUHN), attorneys Sam and Bill Landa, financial advisor Jayson Tanzman, Matt Scarafoni, Colt Insurance Agency, accountant Linda Pruyne, Joanne at Magic Touch Spa, Sauvé Guitars, Yocky Dulcimers, Pohaku Ukuleles, Earnest Instruments, Jim Freeman, Barbara DeMarco, Jess Kielman, Yvonne Pearson and Claire Caeser (Downtown Pittsfield, Inc.), Bill Wilson and staff of the Berkshire Visitors Bureau, Sharon Palma and the staff of the Southern Berkshire Chamber of Commerce, Dave Bissaillion and the staff of the Berkshire Chamber of Commerce, web designer Liz DeMarco (no relation to Barbara).

Gratitude to the Savage family for the perfect place in Pittsfield, MA.

Thanks to my editor, Victoria Wright—great job!

And to Lynne—love trumps everything.

Thank you everyone who played a part, knowingly and unknowingly, in helping me get to this wonderful point in my life.

It took a while.

I am a late bloomer.

***

Expect a miracle!
And, while you're at it, why not expect a few EVERY day?
J.D.P.

***

A MESSAGE FROM JERRY

Are you a "late bloomer?"

Late bloomers, or "elbees" (late bloomer = L.B. = elbee) come in all ages and varieties.

Some bloom at 32, 45, 49, 53, 60, 64 and 87. Others make the breakthrough at 35, 39, 55, 67, 77 and 92.

People have been known to bloom at every age.

Some of us are single, some are married. Some single parents, some married parents. Some of us are rich, some are poor, some are in debt, some are debt-free.
Some live by the beach, some in the city, some in the boonies, some in the 'burbs.

What do we have in common?
Why might we call ourselves *Late Bloomers*?

For some of us, we feel or decide that we haven't
    achieved enough,
    received enough,
    loved enough,
    or succeeded enough.

We might want better ways of dealing with our
    angers,
    guilt,
    frustrations,
    grief,
    sorrows,
    disappointments,

finances,
    relationships.

Possibly, we lost our
    faith,
    hope,
    charity,
    mind,
    luggage.

Or we might desire less
    stress
    clutter
    pain
    nonsense.

Perhaps we want more
    direction,
    satisfaction,
    freedom,
    ease.

Attention late bloomers: it is time to bloom!

Significant positive changes can be made, if the desire is there.

Is it possible? What do *you* think?

DISCLAIMER ET CETERA

It is my pleasure to share the best of what I've learned with you. Be on the lookout for the concepts that are right for you. Different strokes for different folks! And, if your health, psychological, legal, or spiritual problems need professional assistance, please get it and don't wait. This book contains my opinions and observations—all subjective and subject to change. The application of them is your choice and responsibility. The names in my stories may have been changed, and some of my characters might be composites. Please filter my words and ideas through your own life's context and good, old-fashioned "common sense."

Some of the writers and creative beings who influenced my thinking and attitude include, in no particular order: Robert Anton Wilson, Stephen Covey, Frank Zappa, Tony Robbins, Deepak Chopra, Larry Dossey, Louise Hay, The Beatles, Mr. Rogers, Brian Wilson, Lazaris, Dale Carnegie, Julia Cameron, Antero Alli, The Dalai Lama, Jean Shepherd, Cousin Brucie, Mal Sharpe, Devo, Carl Orff, John Cage, Harry Partch, Bob Dylan, Norman Vincent Peale, Alfred E. Newman, Sun Ra, Mike Heron, and Robin Williamson.

My intention is to entertain, educate, enlighten, and inspire positive action on your part!

And you can start some positive action right now, right where you are.

Here's a three-step process for your success:
1. Choose the transformative tools in this book that appeal to you the most.
2. Write them down on little cards or huge posters and read them daily.
3. Act on them.

Thank you.

976-POSI

Back in the 80s, I was associated with a 976 telephone service in Los Angeles. My job was to write a daily two-minute motivational message, and then record it onto the system. People could call and for "$2.00 plus toll if any," they would hear my daily positive boost.

Of course, the customer who benefited the most was probably me. I had to discipline myself to focus on the positive perspective, *daily*, in order to write and record my piece. That regular attention to empowering and transformational words/concepts eventually resulted in increased ability to improve *my* life... and increased ability to ride the ups and downs of life with greater peace, security, and gratitude.

ATTENTION, LATE BLOOMERS: YOU'RE RIGHT ON TIME!

"The ultimate dare is to tell the truth."
   ad for a Madonna movie

"I arise in the morning torn between the desire to improve the world and a desire to enjoy the world."
   E.B. White

THE PRACTICE

When I give a speech or workshop, I often bring my ukulele with me to demonstrate that, with practice, you can become good at something, and without practice, improvement probably will not happen. For positive changes important to me, anything short of daily practice is not an option. The benefits are just too obvious.

Your "practice" is *your choice* of mood-calming, future-causing, success-creating exercises, processes, protocols, reminders, games, or focuses. You might label them spiritual, philosophical, psychological, skills-based... whatever! Remember, it is always *your* choice! You decide what to do, how much to do, and when to do it. You decide how quickly you want (or need) to create positive change.

The yo-yo symbolizes the up and downs of life—that they do happen, and that we've already lived through them and survived. What goes down can, when the cycle turns, come up again. Freaking out at the first sign of adversity isn't a necessity. Simply remembering the yo-yo could trigger a smarter response to challenging situations.

The Native American chief in the popular "Feed the Good Dog" story suggested, "inside of us are two dogs. One mean, evil, pessimistic dog ... and a kind, good, optimistic dog. These dogs are always fighting."

He was asked, "So, if they are always fighting, which one wins?"

"The one I feed more," he replied.

This process is about "feeding the good dog." Focus. Discipline.

Practice. Reinvention. New skills ... and ways to use the old ones better! How to create your daily life in a way that supports your goals, dreams and mental health!

It is possible! Choose "daily practice" that is practical, easy, fun ... and your nervous system will thank you!

HERE'S YOUR MUFFIN!

Before I went to the hospital for a routine procedure well known to middle-aged humans (Okay... it was a colonoscopy), I was told to fast for at least a day, and I did. I arrived at the hospital, got prepped for the procedure, wheeled in, sedated to the point of dreamless nothingness... and the next thing I'm conscious of is a nurse standing in front of me, smiling. I smiled back.

She looked at me, handed me a plate, and said, "Here's your muffin!"

Well, it was *delicious*.

I didn't ask for it. My needs were anticipated and provided for. At that moment, the muffin completely delighted me.

The muffin is my symbol for "that thing we do or give which delights."

If you need permission to accept *your* muffin, or to provide the muffin for your loved ones, customers, clients, vendors, friends, strangers, consider it granted.

Please, consider this story to be your Permission Slip!

NEGATIVE FIBS, POSITIVE TRUTHS—AN EXERCISE

For every negative fib I tell myself, I tell myself three positive truths. That might be something I want to remember: for every negative fib I tell myself, I tell myself three positive truths.

For every negative fib I tell myself, I tell myself three positive truths.

Okay—here's a short pop quiz! Fill in the blank: For every negative fib I tell myself, I tell myself _____ positive truths. Good!

Who *doesn't* have down days? Down days are the best times to do the positive programming and rational thinking. Look at your situation or challenge, and experiment with different interpretations and definitions.

What would be the worst interpretation possible? The very best interpretation possible? How would your best friend define the situation? What would your Future Self suggest? What would Jesus do? Krishna? Buddha? Martin Luther King? Mother Teresa? Condoleezza Rice? Professor Irwin Corey? Albert Einstein? Spiderman? Frank Zappa? Paris Hilton? Pee-Wee Herman?

PEE-WEE

I was living in Southern California in the 80s, determined to "heal my Inner Child" after some life changes, including loss of a job and a divorce. I watched Pee-Wee's Playhouse every week, and considered it cheap therapy. This program had the highest weirdness factor of most anything I've ever seen (which for me, a moon in Aquarius, is high praise). It triggered so many of my own childhood memories and feelings, making it easier to understand how those patterns might still be working in my life.

To music by Devo's Mark Mothersbaugh and legendary recording artist Todd Rundgren, Pee-Wee and his friends—human, plant, animal, machine, and furniture—acted out a very strange and fascinating mixture of classic kid show routines, obvious sexual humor, and wordplay. But the freedom of the Pee-Wee character to be so totally a child, and to have that character accepted and understood by a wildly diverse cast of characters—that is one of the deeper and more profound messages of the show.

The Playhouse was filled with characters playing the parts of traditional archetypes, or "subpersonalities"—the Mother, the Magical Being, the Bully, the Simpleton, the Baby, the Perfect Servant, the Flirt, the Monarch, the Pest.

Might it be that the difference between a good day and a bad one is which subpersonality is doing the interpretation?

19 POSITIVE SUGGESTIONS

1. Pray real hard until you feel better.
2. Take deep breaths. Just breathe, and listen to yourself breathing. Experience the oxygen nourishing your brain and body, calming your entire system. Breathe in, breathe out. In ... out. Yes, there we go ...
3. Clean your bedroom, your bathroom, your desk. Dust your books. Let yourself gaze for a second or two upon each title. What do these books say about *you*? Pick up a favorite book you haven't read for a while, get a nice cup of coffee or tea. Decide to enjoy yourself!
4. Read your journal.
5. Write in your journal.
6. Take a long walk in the woods. Let Mother Nature nurse your wounds.
7. Have a good cry. It's all right. Let it out and let it go.
8. Play pinball and practice psychokinesis.
9. Get your favorite hand puppet and let your negative ego speak through it. Find out what's really going on!
10. Get a collection of Motown dance music from the 60s. Dance your butt off!
11. Look at your astrological transits. Say, "Oh, so *that's* why I'm so freaked out!" Let it be the reason.
12. Frame the events in your life as lessons from a loving and compassionate universe, to you.
13. Go to the mall or outlet village and buy yourself something you really want. Send the other shoppers bright blessings from your heart. Imagine you are a visitor from another planet doing research.
14. Meditate on the future you really, really want!
15. Go to your local costume shop. Rent a costume that best represents your situation. Put on the costume and gaze dispassionately at your reflection in a mirror. Breathe deeply

and allow yourself to slip into an altered state of consciousness. Recognize the unity of all beings, including YOU dressed up like some kind of a nut!

16. Find someone you really, really love, and have fun.

17. Let your Inner Child draw pictures with crayons, or write out his or her feelings. Ask him or her what you can do to assist.

18. Remember: the Path of Life on Earth has ups and downs along the way. Review your victories and strengths. Dwell on the good in your life.

19. BE AT PEACE.

Try this affirmation/reminder: *"I make my choices based on the outcomes I most desire."*

To make this statement operational, first I have to know *the outcomes I most desire.* Maybe I want more happiness. Or better health. Or better financial health. Or clarity of intent. Or a career that I really enjoy, that earns me more than enough money and performs a valuable service.

Am I willing to allow more love in?

Am I willing to change my beliefs?

Am I willing to deserve more?

Am I willing to risk disappointment?

Did I survive disappointments in the past? And am I okay now?

Is the reward worth the risk?

That's the question: *Is the reward worth the risk?*

PROCESSING REJECTION

We might experience rejection in business, in relationships, in the arts. Perhaps our phone calls aren't returned and we feel rejected. We share an idea, and it is rejected by a friend or colleague. Entrepreneurs and salespersons may lose the sale, lose the account, lose the customer, and experience rejection. A friend forgets to call, a letter doesn't come, we take second place in the contest, we're not hired, someone we don't even know looks at us the "wrong way," and we experience rejection!

How to turn feelings of rejection into something positive or productive—can it be done? Feelings, as we suspect, result from thoughts—interpretations of events—that are then labeled "rejection"—triggering yet another series of associated fears, assumptions, made-up stories, etc.

Can I make rejection my ally? Specifically, can I use it for my education? Or, the "every knock is a boost" approach? Can I allow my experience of rejection to make me more sensitive, increase my empathy, and realize that sometimes I, myself, might act as the rejecter?

Can I use rejection as a reminder to refocus on the big picture, and perhaps, take some positive, constructive, miracle-creating action that I might not have taken otherwise? Now we're talking!

Redefining rejection as "simply not the right fit for now" supports a more rational and less painful response. We can use the multi-model approach when we interpret rejection (by a client, customer, prospect, friend, lover) like this:

This rejection could mean _____

_____

Or it could mean _____

_____

Maybe it means this _____

_____

The worst thing that could happen next is _____

_____

The best thing that could happen next is _____

_____

Here's how this might catalyze a miracle _____

_____

When I experience rejection, I can:
    observe my feelings;
    forgive;
    use the multi-model approach;
    learn something valuable from it;
    count my blessings;
    eat an ice cream cone;
    reframe it;
    do the best I can;
    regroup and move forward!

THE POWER OF ONE

How much of our future can we control or create, and how much of it is out of our control? Does a positive, hopeful, loving, grateful attitude increase the likelihood for happiness, health and prosperity? Might a force or power inside of me and outside of me—call it God, Goddess, Higher Intelligence, Higher Power—have some control or influence on the outcome? Can I work with this energy? If the answer is yes, then why don't I work with it more than I do?

So far, decisions I've made, thoughts I've thought, actions I've taken, have "worked" in the sense that I am alive, functional, vital, happy enough, satisfied enough, rich enough, loved enough, loving enough.

I hear a lot of "enoughs" here. Enough for what? How might enough be determined?

WIN with ONE!
Every miracle in your life is the result of gazillions upon gazillions of miracles that precede it. So, by creating "one positive moment" or "one miracle moment" at a time—through willful awareness, willful interpretation, or willful action—we can increase the likelihood of the positive chain reaction that results in miracle after miracle after miracle after miracle. You get the idea!

The application of ONE powerful idea or principle...
ONE key conversation with ONE influential person...
The discipline to focus on ONE daily affirmation...
ONE chance meeting...
ONE lucky break...
ONE kind and generous act...
ONE decision to take the high road...
ONE counterproductive habit broken...
ONE constructive habit made...
ONE miracle...

ONE shift of awareness resulting in an improved point-of-view...

The lives we experience today have been created with a series of "ones"—*one* choice... *one* decision... *one* communication... *one* interpretation... *one* prayer... *one* smile... enjoying *one* really good cup of coffee... *one* kiss... reading *one* great book at the right time... saving *one* inspirational e-mail.

And all of those *ones* add up!

When I want to move into greater love, greater happiness, greater accomplishment, greater awareness, greater abundance and higher consciousness, I find it useful to communicate with the invisible, non-physical Intelligence (which might be addressed as "God" or "The Universe" or whatever feels right for you), as well as addressing my own subconscious/unconscious mind. I like to design my own combination of prayer/affirmations/thought provokers, such as:

- I invite the Universe to utilize my talents and gifts.
- I expect the Universe to delight me with opportunities for growth, success, understanding, peace and service.
- I desire the highest good for my life and the lives of others.
- I imagine my Future Self as happy, secure, confident, abundant, serviceful, even-tempered, loving and well-loved!

I just might be able to further modify my thoughts, feelings and behaviors with esteem-building, perspective-shifting, future-creating, self-fulfilling prophesies, like:

- I am ahead of the curve!
- I shift into hyper-positive mode!
- I am having more fun in my life!
- I am creating a wonderful life.
- I am right where I belong.
- Everything I need is right here.

Now, write a few of your own affirming, esteem-building, perspective-shifting, self-fulfilling prophesy reminders. Write them down on little cards and read them several times daily. Make your choices based on the results you most desire. Consciously focus every day on the results you most desire. That would be ... DAILY! Did I mention "every day?" Review the specific results you most desire—emotionally, materially, spiritually, with people, etc. Daily!

Imagine the results you most desire. Daily!

Expect the results you most desire. Daily!

Affirm the results you most desire. Daily!

Love the results you most desire! Daily!

Put *that* on your to-do list.

ONCE IT'S OUT, YOU CAN'T CONTROL IT

"How many ways can you interpret this moment?"
Jerry Posner

"When someone does something well, applaud! You will make
two people happy."
Samuel Goldwyn

Our words and nonverbal messages, what we say and what we
write—are endowed with a chain-reaction-causing, mystical
life of their own! It never ceases to entertain and astonish me
that the words we say and words we think transform or create "reality"
through associations, assumptions, point-of-view perceptions, etc.

We always communicate *something* (to ourselves, to others, to the
Universe), either consciously or unconsciously. Whether we know it or
not, we're *always* communicating. And, of course, our communications
to others are interpreted through unique nervous system patterns, filters,
and psychology.

Words. Word symbols. Associations. That's what we experience ...
mostly unconsciously, I'd guess. When we say that "our buttons were
pushed" for example, what pushed the button? A word or two? An image
attached to an association? A thought resulting in fear or shame?

I believe that learning to be more aware—to become more conscious
of the words we think and the words we say—will result in more
successes, more peace, and more gratitude. Many of us learn the lessons
of awareness—higher consciousness—by daily practice ... the daily focus
on the positive in some way or another. The positive outlook eventually
becomes automatic; a new and better way of defining situations and
circumstances—our new and improved "default setting" for the nervous
system.

For example, you can start the day by writing a two minute positive
message to yourself. Something like:

There are things I can do, thoughts I can think, words I can say that could make this day a truly wonderful day. I choose to focus on gratitude, peace, and the best ways I can be of service to myself and others.

I am on the lookout for thoughts and words that could sabotage my success and happiness. I notice them and change them into positive, accurate, life-affirming thoughts.

I am a "word-magician," making "thought-magic" with the conscious application of what seems to be a collection of mostly commonsense techniques.

The power of words. *So* powerful! Change the words... change your life!

Yesterday, I gave a seminar for unmarried people. I asked, "What words would you use to describe your current situation?" Some examples I gave were: single, unpartnered, and in between relationships.

It was cool to see people's mood, look, and energy change when they went from being single to being in between relationships! One can go from lonely to enjoying solitude in a heartbeat.

Are you unemployed or in between gigs?

Weird or unique or avant-garde or nonconformist or creative genius or innovative independent thinker ...?

Pushy or assertive or willful or strong leader or "I know who I am and what I want" or "I get what I want" or focused?

Does *every* word and word formula trigger a corresponding, unique-to-me, mental, emotional and spiritual condition? It seems so to me, that our own choices of definitions and unconscious associations do indeed regulate our reality concept and thus our choices and behavior.

So, if we want to, we can become more aware of our own self-definitions and self-talk—and perhaps change or upgrade the language to more empowering and rational language than we're currently using!

For example:

I am living the life I chose, I will live the life I choose. I attract to me the conditions for my happiness. I am more and more aware of my needs, wants and preferences. I freely forgive myself and others, because I want to! I have permission to love and appreciate my life. I have permission to add value to my life and work. I can make my choices based on the emotional, material, financial, and social outcomes I most desire.

I check in with my needs, wants and preferences daily. I influence outcomes with my thoughts, feelings, and actions.

I am connected to Higher Intelligence, Higher Love, and Higher Consciousness, and I remember and honor those connections.

THE FUTURE-SELF

Modern theories of quantum physics, as well as ancient spiritual and metaphysical schools, suggest that past, present and future all exist, in some form, all at the same "time."

You might have experienced "all time is now" yourself. Perhaps during meditation, while at prayer, when having a déjà vu or synchronicity experience, you *felt* or *knew* that you were modifying or healing or influencing your past, present and future—all at once!

Think about *your* future, now.
Clarify the future you most want to participate in.
Imagine *yourself* in that future.
Mentally rehearse it... *every* day.
Feel the feelings associated with your optimal future... daily.

Think about your future, *now*.
Clarify the future you *most* want to participate in!
Imagine yourself in *that* future.
Mentally *rehearse* it... every day.
Feel the feelings associated with your *optimal* future... daily.

Different Emphasis... Different Meaning!

One theory: Attention promotes change on a subatomic level, which simultaneously affects the atomic level, which then has an impact on the molecular level, which could determine whether or not you have a happy day!

Here are some examples of positive future-self affirmations/self-talk:

My Future-Self experiences joy, happiness, and emotional security.
My Future-Self behaves rationally and intelligently.

My Future-Self often feels gratitude, peace, and appreciation.
My Future-Self has the freedom to create a wonderful life.
My Future-Self has meaningful, fun, profitable, serviceful work.
My Future-Self sees the Big Picture and releases all grudges.
My Future-Self is brave, kind, compassionate, and generous.

Now, jot down a few characteristics of *your* Future-Self !

My Future-Self experiences _____

_____

My Future-Self feels _____

_____

My Future-Self has _____

_____

My Future-Self sees _____

_____

What do you think will happen to you, if you review your list every day, and edit it as you see fit?

THE CARE AND FEEDING OF BABY WANNA

"WAHHHHHHHH!"
"I *want!*"
"*I* want!!"
"I WAAAAAANNNNTTTT!!!"

That is the unmistakable sound of Baby Wanna. Do you have a Baby Wanna within, who makes a dramatic appearance in the outer world from time to time?

Being a baby, Baby W. is not expected to understand or process information as an adult might. Some of Baby Wanna's "wants" are downright unreasonable! Therefore, rather than allow Baby Wanna to "drive the bus" (make the decisions), it might be smarter for our "adult selves" to supervise, tutor, and nurture our still active "baby selves."

Sometimes, we might be unconsciously compensating for what we think we lacked as a child, with behavior that isn't all that cool for someone over the age of eleven. *Oh, nooooooooooo!* It is helpful to know the difference between Baby Wanna's wants (based on the past hurts, fears, child point-of-view), and the wants of the enlightened, aware, functional adult (that's you and I, in the present).

I have found "Inner Child Work" or "Healing the Inner Child" protocols *extremely* transformational and practical. A simple version is: relax, close your eyes, imagine yourself (the adult) having a visit with yourself as a child, maybe five or seven years old.

In your imagination, ask how you can help him or her. What are the needs of this child? What "boo-boos" need kissing? And in your imagination, since you have an unlimited expense account there, you can give that child whatever his or her heart desires. Imagine the child (you) actually having the magical powers, the parental love in the preferred style, the right toys, caring friends, acceptance and security, the fame and fortune, the skills for success... anything!

And you can honestly say to that child (in your imagination, in meditation), "I am your Future-Self. We turned out okay! There is nothing to worry about. Gimme five!!"

A daily "Inner Child" session works on many levels, beginning a chain reaction that could result in more confidence, less conflict, more self-awareness, better and better decisions... many improvements!

So, thank you Baby Wanna, for bringing my previously hidden needs to my conscious attention, so I can respond to them in a practical way— in meditation, in my inner world, which is where the pattern resides.

IS CHANGE YOUR ALLY?

"If you're going through hell, keep going."
Sir Winston Churchill

Given the state of being human, and the nature of life on Earth, I'd say that making change your ally is a smart move. Yet, change is typically interpreted as scary, unsettling, or stressful, even if the change has more potential upside than downside.

Yes, the change turns out for the better, and we've wasted all of that high-quality angst and anxiety... for nothing! How we view and interpret the change and what we do after the change may be more important that the change itself.

There are many categories of change. Some we control, some are beyond our control. Some we manage, some we cope with, some we adapt to, some we initiate: change of attitude; change of mood; change of employment or clients or customers; change of style; change of relationships; change of financial circumstances; change of health; wellness, vitality; change of diet; change of residence; change of behavior; change of underwear...

I had the pleasure of interviewing Mal Sharpe, a brilliant and kind San Francisco-based radio personality, practicing Buddhist and recording artist. He was best known for "man-on-the-street" put-ons that were both avant-garde and enlightening. In one routine, on his album *The Meaning of Life*, Mal advocated changing underwear several times daily, to remind one that change is the order of the universe. "Change your underwear and change your life!" Philosophical prank as it was, the concept is solid.

Regularly remind yourself that change can be good and you will probably experience less stress and anxiety when a change occurs. You might even set some causes into motion that will result in *very* positive changes for you... and everyone you affect!

Try these affirmations for positive change for yourself. Once a day, say them and see how they might guide and improve your relationship to change:

I make the most of my changes.

I choose to see the positive potential when changes happen.

I embrace change.

Change is my friend.

I love change, and change loves me.

I make change my ally.

I change my mind... and keep the change!

10 Simple Suggestions to Help You Catalyze POSITIVE CHANGES in Your Life

1. Define the positive changes you want the most, and write them down. Study your list every day. Edit as necessary.
2. Examine your attitudes and commitment to making those changes.
3. Carefully consider the impact that these changes will have on your life. Project yourself into the future and have a look around!
4. Visualize (imagine) the final results you want. At least twice daily. Did I mention daily? That would be *every* day!
5. Write down five things you're grateful for, daily. Big deals, small blessings, deep or trivial ... just do it every day!
6. Ask for and accept help when you need it. Prayer, Google.com, support from friends, networking ...
7. Use your "to-do" list to reinforce your desire to make the changes. Remind yourself that you're serious.
8. Give yourself permission to succeed at this process. Write yourself a "permission slip!"
9. Have more fun with this process then you think you're supposed to. That's right. FUN. JOY. HAPPINESS.
10. Be mindful of results. Notice what's working and what isn't. Modify your plan as necessary.

In the stock market and in life ...

Patience, flexibility, optimism and research is necessary.

Sometimes you get lucky ... sometimes you make your own luck!

Listen to the buzz, make your own decisions.

Take responsibility for those decisions. Look for causes and effects. The more you play, the better you get.

Surprises and shocks happen to everyone.

Lose and win with dignity. Perfectionism guarantees disappointment.

Don't worry—be grateful!

RIGHT PLACE ... RIGHT TIME!

I've heard that the term "synchronicity" comes from Swiss psychologist Carl Jung and, translated from the Latin, literally means "joined with time."

The concept of synchronicity implies an invisible intelligence or energy that connects everything and is sometimes revealed through a meaningful coincidence or miracle—being in the right place at the right time for a desired (or sometimes novel) result.

How do synchronicities work? How do they happen? Well, that would depend on your favorite model. There are countless spiritual, metaphysical, scientific, psychological, neurological, and philosophical models for how and why synchronicities happen.

Rather than pondering their mechanics or inventing more definitions, I am much more interested in having more of them! After all, synchronicities are fun, fascinating, and make us *really think* about how things work. A good synchronicity will blow your mind... and blow a hole in your reality-concept!

Like finding lucky pennies, I think we can surely experience more synchronicities by thinking about them more, wanting them more, expecting to have them, expecting to notice them, reminding ourselves that they *can* happen, and that they *do* happen!

We tend to notice what we repeatedly look for, right? (That sounds like something Yogi Berra might have said). A great way to experience/notice more synchronicities is to keep a Synchronicity Journal. Whenever I observe a synchronicity in my own life, or when I hear about a really good one, I write about it. I keep a record.

Here are some excerpts from my own Synchronicity Journal:

I had a brief, fleeting thought about my cousin, whom I haven't been in contact with for, oh, at least twenty or thirty years. *The day after I thought about him*, he IM'ed me when I was online. He found me with a Google search, checked out my website, and got my screen name.

I was in Gloucester, Massachusetts for the first time. My friend gave me directions to her summer home on Bungalow Road, but left out an important turn, so I was going in circles for forty-five minutes. I finally decided to stop at a fire station to ask for directions. The moment my hand knocked the door, the fire alarm went off and the little loudspeaker began to broadcast, "Go to Bungalow Road ... Bungalow Road!"

I asked if I could follow them and they said that they'd be going too fast, but they gave me the real directions. So, I proceeded to the house, found it without any problem, and found the door locked.

A few seconds later, my friend's assistant ran up to the house with the key. Out of breath, she said, "I'm so sorry. Were you waiting long? I fell asleep on the beach and the fire engine's siren woke me up!"

I had just moved to Pittsfield, Massachusetts and I knew just one person in the whole town, the woman who owned Crystal Works on North Street. We had been talking about guitars and I mentioned to her that I especially loved Gibson acoustic guitars. I was about to leave when she asked me if I could stay a few minutes longer and watch the store while she went to the bathroom.

"Sure," I said.

The phone rang, I answered, and a guy asked, "Do you buy musical instruments?"

I said, "The store doesn't, but I might, what do you have?"

"A 12-string Gibson acoustic—in a very good hard case!"

He brought it in, and I offered $50.00 cash (which was what I had on me).

To my amazement, he said, "Well, I'm leaving for Colorado tomorrow and I can't take it with me. OK, you can have it for $50.00. Congratulations!"

I was teaching a workshop at Canyon Ranch in Lenox, Massachusetts. I mentioned that I once lived on Commonwealth Ave in Boston. After the class, a man asked me what number Commonwealth Ave.

"386," I said.

"That's amazing," he said, "my company is renovating that very building. We practically tore it down."

We talked a bit more and he asked me if that was where I lived when I want to college.

"No," I said, "I lived on a little street near Huntington Ave., behind the Stop and Shop called Burbank St."

"What number?" he asked.

"70."

The guy stared at me... his company was renovating that building, also.

I couldn't find my gloves, thinking that I might have left them in a friend's car earlier that day. It was a cold night, and I needed to get my own car which I had parked at the hotel a few blocks from my apartment.

I was about to leave when my phone rang. It was a wrong number.

Then the phone rang again. It was the same wrong number.

I finally walked out the door and, as I did, my friends drove by, saw me, and stopped.

Amazed to see them, I asked, "Did I leave my gloves in your car?"

I did! If I didn't get the two wrong numbers, I would have missed them.

A woman I met told me that she was riding her bicycle in a fundraiser for the Muscular Dystrophy Association. She took a bad spill and limped to the nearest house. A woman answered the door and helped her with her wounds. They got to talking and the bicycle rider told the woman what she was doing. The woman started to cry. She had been diagnosed with muscular dystrophy the day before.

I was walking by the Crowne Plaza Hotel when I found a cell phone by the sidewalk, in the snow. I picked it up, held it, and wondered, "What is the best thing to do?"

I thought about bringing it to the hotel's front desk, or just leaving it there. I was not sure what action to take, so I just stood there for what must have been three or four minutes. I then decided to bring it to the hotel ... and that was when I saw the guy running down the block toward where I was standing. I held up the phone. It was his!

I was fifteen years old and hanging out in Greenwich Village, NYC. A guitar in a second-hand shop on Sixth Avenue caught my eye. At the time, I did not play or own a guitar, but I wanted to, and this guitar was gorgeous! It was only $30.00, but I had $11.00 in my pocket, which included my subway and bus money. I walked to Washington Square Park and sat by the fountain, thinking about the guitar. I *really* wanted that guitar!

As I sat, imagining myself playing that guitar, the strong wind was blowing leaves and papers all around. I noticed a little piece of paper that the wind delivered right to my feet. It was money! A folded up ten-dollar bill! I picked it up, unfolded it ... and found that another bill was folded into it. A twenty!

I ran all the way back to the store and bought my first guitar with the exact amount of money that somehow came to me that day. The *exact* amount!

Can you remember a few excellent synchronicities you've experienced? Jot them down, and begin your own Synchronicity Journal.

I can write and recite Synchronicity Affirmations, such as:

I alert my nervous system to be on the lookout for synchronicities.
I create and notice positive synchronicities.
My life is filled with wonderful synchronicities.
I am "in sync" with the positive, creative energy flow.
I am allowed to have many excellent synchronicities.
I am in the right place at the right time.
I pray for synchronicities.
I love synchronicities.

GETTING UNSTUCK

"When I do good, I feel good. When I do bad, I feel bad. And that's my religion. "
Abraham Lincoln

"While we have the gift of life, it seems to me the only tragedy is to allow part of us to die, whether it is our spirit, our creativity, or our glorious uniqueness."
Gilda Radner

Having emotional challenges? Temporarily stuck in a crappy belief system? Complaining a little more than you'd like to be? Is self-pity showing his/her ugly face again? ("I thought I was *over* that!")

Do you remember how you successfully processed or reframed the challenging issue in the past? Remember how you were able to snap yourself out of it before?

Did you utilize creative visualization and prayer? Positive affirmations? Maybe a trip to the coffee shop for a triple-caffeine-brain-shaker (with soy milk) and a biscotti? Perhaps you dusted off your gratitude journal and made up for lost time by writing down one hundred things you're grateful for, or grabbed a legal pad and listed one hundred reasons to let go and move on.

I have found it extremely helpful to observe my problem or situation from a few different points of view.

For example:

First, I clearly state the problem or difficulty. (My employer called me a slacker and threatened to fire my sorry ass, which made me feel like a slug!)

Next, I describe it in a *different* way. (The need for career improvement was brought to my attention. I could act on this practical suggestion, increasing my market value, self-esteem, and maturity. Perhaps I am not communicating the right messages to the guy who writes my paycheck ... perhaps I need to.)

Then I state it in *still another* way. (The boss seemed to be having a tough day, which I certainly understand, as he's been under a lot of pressure lately. I'm going to get him a latte. Ah, yes. Another excellent opportunity to express compassion and nonattachment, as I progress on my Path of Buddhahood.)

Finally, I describe it in yet *one more different* way. (Perhaps the Universe is sending me a signal for a career change.)

So, tell me. What's the problem?

State the problem or difficulty clearly:_____
_____

Now, describe it in a different way:_____
_____

State it in still another way:_____
_____

Last, describe it in yet one more different way:_____
_____

Good work! Okay, now write down ten things (circumstances, conditions, situations, material things, relationships) in your life right now for which you are truly and deeply grateful.

1._____
2._____
3._____
4._____
5._____
6._____
7._____
8._____
9._____
10._____

If you skipped this exercise, please go back and *do* it!

Excellent! Now imagine you have a Good Angel on your shoulder. This angel can look like Jesus, Buddha, Bob Marley, Frank Zappa, Albert Einstein, Bessie Smith, George Burns, Betty Boop, Jerry Garcia, John Lennon, Aunt Blanche, Gandhi, Martin Luther King, Elvis, Bob Dylan, a hero, a loved one, a saint, a media celebrity—maybe even your old guru or boss! Your choice.

The angel asks you, "Are you choosing optimism or pessimism?"
And you answer, "I choose optimism (or pessimism) because _____

_____

_____

Then the angel asks, "Why are you making these choices?"
And you answer, "I make my choices because _____

_____

_____

So the angel asks, "How do you think the Universe operates, anyway?"
And you answer, "I think the Universe operates in the way I think because_____

_____

_____

Finally, the angel asks, "Why do you think that you see the Universe the way you do?"
And you answer, "I see the Universe the way I do because _____

_____

_____

Now the angel is silent, so you can think about your answers. By the way, there are no wrong answers here!

YOU AND YOUR MIRACLES, PART ONE

"To see things in the seed, that is genius."
   Lao-Tzu

"The winds of grace are blowing all the time. You have only to raise your sail."
   Ramakrishna

Miracle, noun. From Latin miraculum: object of wonder; *mirari:* to wonder at; *mirus:* astonishing, wonderful thing

The word "miracle" is used in many contexts—from the very sacred and rare to a type of salad dressing. We see the word in song, film, and book titles. We have miracle healings, miracle drugs, miracle washday detergents, Smokey Robinson and the Miracles.

So, what *is* a miracle? Is a miracle something supernatural, or do miracles happen every moment? Is childbirth a miracle? Winning the lottery or picking a stock that doubles in value? How about the way our atoms, molecules and cells function? Is gravity a miracle? How about soulmates finding each other?

I had a near-death experience on June 29, 1976. Before that event, I didn't consider that my life contained too many miracles. After that event, I perceived the sun, the trees, my breathing, the movement of my arms and legs—all of these and more—to be "miracles!" What changed?

Albert Einstein is quoted as having said something like, "There are two ways to live: you can live as if nothing is a miracle; you can live as if everything is a miracle." I say "something like" because I have seen at least four versions. I believe that Dr. Einstein was referring to point of view... perspective... interpretation... definitions... the "glasses" or "filters" through which we observe the world.

Some simply define "miracle" as a positive event or situation that *seems* against the odds (low probability from our point of view) that can happen, or does happen. *Really* good luck! The "Speedi Index" version of Webster's Dictionary defines "miracle" as an "unusual, splendid occurrence." I like that. If you have a broad definition of "miracle" you will probably get more of them!

Let's look at that definition as a starting point. "Unusual" must certainly be seen in context. What is unusual for you, might not be unusual for me. What was unusual for you as a child, might not be unusual for you as an adult. What was unusual for someone living in the 18th century might not be unusual for George Jetson.

"Splendid" seems like a no-brainer. "Splendid" clearly means "excellent." However, I think some of our greatest miracles can be born out of adversity or tragedy. We lose our job, for example, and we're angry, hurt, confused, freaked out, scared, depressed. Then, perhaps, we find a better job, or start our own business, or learn something important about ourselves. Now, we have a new trajectory, new awareness, a new life which never would have happened if we hadn't been kicked out of our comfort zone. So the bad thing becomes the catalyst for the miracle!

The loss of a marriage might result in a better marriage. A stock market crash might result in new values, priorities, and less attachment to the material world ... which then has a ripple (or domino or butterfly) effect that reverberates on into infinity.

Sometimes a personal tragedy impels us to become stronger, more loving, more compassionate, more giving, kinder, more mindful, more grateful, more heroic ... and changes us for the better, forever. Now, we are making better choices, communicating differently, behaving differently, seeing our lives in a new and more empowering context.

Clearly, some miracles are gifts. We do not consciously participate in their creation. They come to us, or are arranged for us, somehow. I have heard the term "deliverance miracle" referring to the near-miss scenario.

One account of a deliverance miracle is the well-documented, oft-told tale of the church choir in Beatrice, Nebraska. The facts as reported are these: Choir practice at the West Side Baptist Church in Beatrice, began at 7:20 on Wednesday evenings. There were fifteen members of the choir, from ten households. On Wednesday, March 1, 1950, one member of the choir was going to be late due to a car not starting. Another would be late because of a nap that lasted a little too long. A compelling radio drama delayed two other members, while geometry homework was delaying another. At 7:25 PM, Wednesday, March 1, 1950, a freak explosion, believed to be caused by a gas leak, destroyed the church. Windows in nearby homes were shattered and a nearby radio station was taken off the air by the blast. The fifteen members of the choir, usually prompt, were *all* late that one night due to seemingly unrelated circumstances. The church was empty, no one was harmed.

How did something like this happen? *LIFE* magazine reported that choir members considered divine intervention as a possible explanation. Some might say, "really good luck" or "amazing coincidence!" Others might cite theories of quantum physics, metaphysics, karma, fate...

The purpose and mechanics of deliverance miracles are highly speculative to me. Your interpretation would depend on your world view, religious or metaphysical training, or beliefs. I am much more interested in the kind of "miracles" we can consciously participate in the creation of.

"If you could create a miracle in your life ... what might it be?" I have been pondering that exact question for over twelve years. In fact, since 1994 I have written that question on white boards and flip charts more than five hundred times, at my "Ways to Create Miracles in Your Life" workshops and speeches. I have developed a three-step process that has proved to be practical and valuable for those who wish to create a specific miracle or to become more miracle-prone.

YOU AND YOUR MIRACLES, PART TWO

"It's not what you look at that matters, it's what you see..."
Henry David Thoreau

STEP ONE: Choose a miracle to create!

This miracle can be a tiny miracle, a small miracle, a medium-sized miracle, a large, an extra-large or a *huge* miracle. It can be a project already in progress or process, or it can be something new.

Your miracle can be labeled a goal or a hope or a dream or an objective if you would like. It obviously must be possible (has anyone else ever made a similar miracle?). You really, *really*, **really** have to want it, and be willing to work for it. Yes, miracles do require some work!

There are accomplishment miracles, healing miracles, business and career miracles, financial miracles, emotional management miracles, stress management miracles.

Like goals, there are short-term, medium-term and long-term miracles. Often, what we prefer as short-term miracles turn out to be medium-term or even long-term miracles! This is fine. Patience is often required, as we will discuss.

You can consider that your miracle is a positive change of some kind—materially, financially, emotionally, behaviorally, situationally—that *seems* to be of low probability to you, or that you're not sure how to achieve, or that you've tried before and failed so that now you say, "*That* would be a *miracle*!"

Perhaps it is a relationship miracle—creating, dissolving, healing, fixing, reconciling, or otherwise modifying a relationship you have to another person.

Your miracle might have to do with your behavior. Maybe you wish to express more kindness, more gratitude, more love. Or, you have a behavior habit that is clearly destructive, and you'd like to stop it.

Your miracle might have to do with your perceptions or beliefs.

Maybe you wish to see the world in a more empowering way, or you have beliefs that are clearly destructive, and you'd like to stop them. Perhaps your miracle is to be more optimistic, have more faith, update your basic values.

Remember—each and every miracle begins a new chain reaction that goes on into infinity!

Look at your life as it is now. How many miracles did it take to get you from an egg and a sperm to where you are sitting now? Was it a miracle that your mom and dad met, and that they liked each other, at least enough (and long enough), to create you? Was it a miracle that your grandparents or great-grandparents or great-great-grandparents made certain decisions that eventually resulted in *you*, reading these words today?

Okay, now pick a miracle to create. You can change it later if you want to.

My miracle is _____

_____

STEP TWO: Understand what you want!

Next, we want to *aim* at the future that contains the miracle! If we had a bow and arrow, and we wanted to hit the target's bull's eye with the arrow, we would have to aim at the target, focus on the bull's eye, and shoot the arrow in that direction.

Of course, we sometimes do just the opposite. We say we want to lose ten pounds, yet we visit Ben and Jerry regularly (and I don't mean the frozen yogurt). We say we want to be a great musician, but we never practice. We say we want fame and fortune, but we're afraid of fame and don't think we deserve fortune! Single people might say they want to be married, but run (real fast) in the opposite direction at the first sign of a blooming love!

It is very important to understand our relationship to this thing that we say that we want. We want to examine our attitudes and motives, making sure that the miracle is appropriate for us now, and that we are willing to resolve any conflicts that might interfere.

We want to AIM at the future that contains the miracle!

A.I.M. Attitude. Impact. Motivation.

YOU AND YOUR MIRACLES, PART THREE

"Good habits are as addictive as bad habits, and a lot more rewarding."
Harvey Mackay

How do you create a miracle? Well, how do you create *anything*? Let's consider these three areas:

1.   Habits
2.   Choices
3.   ? ? ?

Habits are things we do, thoughts we think, ways that we process and interpret information, words we say that are automatic—often without any awareness whatsoever. We might not remember where or when the habit was formed, but it was... and it is still running!

Naturally, we have *good*, *bad*, and *neutral* habits. If your habits get you from where you are to where you want to be—if your habits bring you what you want, promote the states of consciousness and health you desire—then we say, "*Good* habit!"

Do you question your bad habits? Ever ask yourself, "Why, exactly, do I believe this crap about myself?" Or, "Why, exactly, do I do this ridiculously unproductive act over and over and over again?"

The act of questioning activates the power of choice. Choice implies awareness and consciousness. Let's see... I can turn left, or turn right. I can behave kindly or meanly. I can forgive or hold a grudge. I can do my work or goof off. I can think positively or think negatively—that is choice.

I create miracles with certain habits. I create miracles with certain choices.

The third component, "???" has to do with our personal connection to the invisible world—the unseen—how we relate to it and how we manage it. This includes God/Goddess, Higher Self, Higher Intelligence (and brain functions of all varieties), angels, religion, metaphysics, prayer, astrology, psychic phenomena, karma, etc. Whatever works for you. It's your choice (and there's that word again!). I use the question marks because the exact nature of our spiritual or metaphysical nature and practice can seem mysterious and mystical, and certainly quite varied from person to person. So, to make the miracle, we want to have our habits, choices, and spirituality/metaphysics all working in the same direction without conflict.

STEP THREE: Apply one or more of the Miracle Creating Tools every day. That would be ... daily!

In my study of people who made miracles—miracle healings, miracle careers, miracle transformations—I noticed certain patterns. Miracle makers regularly applied "inner tools" that motivated or resulted in positive changes, outer actions, and eventually, the miracle.

Posner's Seven Tools for Creating Miracles

1. **Imagine it daily.** Visualize the final results of the miracle as vividly as possible. Imagine the details, the sounds, the smells. Imagine it being solid and real!
2. **Desire it daily.** Embrace your goal with your feelings. Feel the feelings associated with the goal. Focus! Think of a two-year-old who wants a cookie. He or she does not see any separation between the mouth and the cookie The kid is already "one with the cookie!" Feel the emotional fulfillment of the miracle in advance.
3. **Anticipate it daily.** Don't worry, obsess, complain, or fret. Be patient. Have faith. Live *as if* the miracle is, indeed, being created. Have "hope by choice."
4. **Ask for assistance.** In business, we call it networking. If you are religious, pray. Ask for and accept emotional, spiritual, and material assistance, if appropriate, from supportive friends, family, and allies. Need information? Ask Google.com! Some miracles are achieved by telling *everyone* what you need... some miracles are private. Know the difference—do not share your miracle with people who will ridicule you or put a negative spin on it.

5.   Put your miracle at the top of your "to do" list. Make sure you remind yourself of your miracle several times every day. Of course, if you are habituated to completing the tasks on your list, then you will surely take the steps to make your miracle. "Its on my list, I *have* to do it!" Some miracles are so important that you will remember them anyway. Some miracles need the daily reminder or reinforcement in order to be created by you.

6.   Practice optimism by choice—*all the time.* Sometimes we have to be militant with our optimism. Do not allow negativity to win! Both optimism and pessimism are creative energies that will create—or at the very least—influence the outcome. Become aware of any mixed messages you are giving yourself— and stop! Be 100% positive about your miracle. Yes, you do risk disappointment, but know that the optimistic attitude will increase the likelihood of your success.

7.   Give yourself permission to have your miracle. Write yourself a "permission slip!" Affirm that you deserve, and you are allowed to have, your miracle. I'm told that, for many people, this is a huge key. The blockage to your miracle just might be ... you!

By the way, you do not have to be a perfect person in order to create your miracle. *One hundred percent* of the people I've interviewed or studied who made their miracles were not perfect people! Design a custom miracle-making daily program for yourself ... and have fun making your miracles.

A B CS

Allow yourself to have more fun, peace, pure joy and appreciation!

Believe that you can do it.

Choose the route that leads to the destination of your choice!

Define and delineate that which you most desire. Determine to dock with your dearest destiny.

Every day!

Focus on the positive future you wish to create.

Greet your optimal future ... as your optimal future greets you.

Harm no one. Happy. Healthy. Hi-dee-hi ... Hi-dee-ho!

I am affirming the future I desire to create.

In my mind ... positive thoughts.

Just once or twice a day should do it!

Keep focused and on track.

Let bygones be bygones.

Learn your lessons!

Make choices based on the outcomes you most desire.

Notice the miracles in your life.

Observe your emotions with calm compassion.

Opportunities for growth and bliss exist every moment.

Pick a peck of possible, positive interpretations.

Process and program consciously and carefully.

Quit your old and useless habits.

Review, reinforce and remember your goals.

Stop all unnecessary worrying.

Take a "gratitude break" now.

Understand your unique, personal life-path.

Vote for the positive reality of your choice.

Walk your path with dignity, joy, and awareness.

X-factors must be figured in to life's equations!

You are the sunshine ... the glowing potential ... the bright light.

Zero is wasted, all is grist for the mill.

THE POSNERIAN TIMES IS BORN

"... a rapidly growing newsletter dedicated to positive reality creation, rapid personal growth and transformation, fun on the Path, and NETWORKING, PROSPERITY, FREEDOM AND LOVE."

I moved from Southern California to the Berkshires in July of 1989, living in Don and Jackie Wescott's log cabin, and thinking that I'd eventually get a radio gig in a major market. I read the weekly want ads in *Broadcasting* and *Radio and Records*; recorded and mailed out audition tapes with my resume. I needed to stay positive and optimistic in the face of the uncertainty of job hunting, so I worked with positive affirmations. I made lists of them, recited them, and made recordings of them (playing them continually). This helped.

I remember taking large sheets of art paper and making posters of positive sayings, thought provokers and affirming concepts. I wanted to *totally* immerse myself in positivity, since I was prone to ... well, just the opposite!

Here are some examples of what I called *Posi-Posters*:

THINK YOU'RE NOT CREATIVE?
YOU'RE CREATING THE FUTURE, RIGHT NOW!

I AM FOCUSED ON MY POSITIVE GOALS

PESSIMISM SUCKS!
OPTIMISM MAKES MIRACLES ... and love conquers all.

When adversity strikes –
that's when the learning gets deeper.

I AM SUCCEEDING.

I VISUALIZE HAPPY ENDINGS

I did visualize happy endings, but I didn't know the actual *form* they would take. I used to imagine myself being happy, healthy, and working in a career that I would: enjoy, make a good living with, be proud of, and had *real* value and purpose. I would "see" myself smiling, with money in my pocket and a feeling of fulfillment and accomplishment.

Yet, when I did hear back from a radio station, it was a rejection.

As my money ran out, and the holiday season approached, my old boss Ron Straile got in touch with me. He hired me to interview, train, and supervise a sales force to sell jewelry in an eighteen minute presentation (that's like "buy one ... and get one free! But, *wait* ... there's MORE!!!") in military base exchanges in Texas, Oklahoma, Mississippi, Georgia, Maine, Rhode Island... So, I was off!

The woman I hired for the Newport Navy Exchange fainted after her debut, so I ended up doing the gig in December, 1989. Returning to the log cabin and finding it unfit for winter occupancy, freezing my butt off, I was invited to stay with Don and Jackie in Natick, Massachusetts.

Don had a Mac Plus computer with an external 20 meg hard drive and, I believe, 2 megs of RAM, which by today's standards, was an absurdly small amount of storage and memory. I spent the first part of 1990 learning how to operate it. Using a primitive SuperPaint program, I made word collages and "posi-posters" again, to remind myself to stay optimistic.

Wanting to stay in touch with my friends in California, learn the computer, and stay positive ... I decided to publish a small magazine. I called it *The Posnerian Times*. It was a pretty strange looking mix of positive philosophy and over-the-top typography that harked back to comic books, Dr. Bronner's soap labels, and those weird little ads in the back of Popular Science from the 1950s.

From *The Posnerian Times*, Spring 1990:

To your Inner Child ... you *are* the future!
Posi-Tip: Make a list of all the humiliating experiences you had in

school, grades K through 9, especially. Look at them without too much judgment! Try to feel the feelings again. Love that little guy or girl no matter what! See how you can change the past!

The more positive techniques and technology you have access to, the easier and more fun the Path becomes. The goal of the Path is growth. We can learn to realize it every single day. It is possible to accelerate the process, and have a wonderful time doing it! The more positive input you accept, the better your life will be. You can choose your beliefs when you see that it is *possible* and worth the effort. We need to be aware of our beliefs, watch 'em operate, and improve 'em. Change the ones that bring you misery. Change the ones that feel terrible. Modify outdated data. If you are satisfied with your program, great! If not, you can change the program. That is what *The Posnerian Times* is all about.

Young, old, Christian, Jew, Pagan, Earth-based or Extraterrestrial... welcome!

Words are drugs, so get high on the positive and empowering word-drugs found in this publication. Explore new and happier ways to express yourself. Let us wash your brain for you—absolutely free!

POSI-YOGA 101

Negative Ego Scripts to Watch

1. "I'm not mad. Why should I be mad? I'm not angry. I never get angry."
2. "I don't need to be aware or responsible now. I can be aware or responsible later."
3. "How come all of these terrible things happen to *me?*"
4. "Nobody *really* cares about my feelings."
5. "It is too hard to be so damn *positive*. What's wrong with being negative? It's only polarity, it's the same thing. Open, closed—what's the damn difference anyway? It's just *your* belief system!"

Reality Theories/Reality Choices

1. We consciously create our very own reality.
2. "Reality" is a plural noun.
3. The words we use to describe reality actually determine the nature of reality.
4. There are many possible realities, and we have the ability to choose the better ones, even though our subconscious programming sometimes picks lousy ones.
5. If you can imagine it, you can achieve it.
6. If you can imagine it, you can create it.
7. If you can imagine it, you can be it.
8. Parts of the mind cannot tell the difference between what happened in reality and what was vividly imagined.
9. It is possible to pull a little switcheroo!

We can't suppress our problems forever. It just ain't healthy! If you hurt, you hurt. No real reason to lie to yourself about it. Just because you got hurt in the past does not mean that hurt must exist in the future.

Let us now create a future with less hurt, more compassion, more fun and less ego crap. Let's do it together! We can link up, in spirit, with hundreds of thousands of positive thinking and feeling people all over the world.

Say *yes* to the Self you know is Real.
Say *yes* and allow yourself to heal.
Say *yes* to love and positive change.
Say *yes* to positive moods maintained.
Say *yes* to prosperity and big bucks.
Say *yes* to Self-created good luck.

THE MAGIC BLUE DOT

"Pessimists calculate the odds. Optimists believe they can overcome them."
   Ted Koppel

"I have tried 99 times and have failed, but on the 100th time came success."
   Albert Einstein

Have you ever seen the "Magic Blue Dot" in the *National Enquirer*? Also known as the "*Lucky* Blue Dot," this circle-on-newsprint (and sometimes on small cards) ranges in size from a silver dollar to a large peppermint patty. In the newspaper, it was strongly suggested that this piece of paper, operated correctly, has the power to help you get what you want in life.

I have read stories of people, who, after properly rubbing the Blue Dot, were quoted as saying that the Blue Dot played a key role in their successes—monetary and otherwise.

How does it work? The newspaper reported that two women with psychic skills performed an energy ritual of sorts on the Blue Dot, so when you or I rub, or simply hold the image of the Blue Dot in our hand, while vividly imagining (perhaps hoping for, praying for) the desired creation, manifestation, or circumstance ... it will come! It will happen! There appears to be evidence to support this theory.

Is the Blue Dot a cost-effective placebo?

Is the Blue Dot a reminder to "think positive"?

Is the Blue Dot a simple tool for focusing mental/emotional/spiritual energy?

Is the Blue Dot really magical? Did the two psychics actually influence the time-space continuum with their well-intentioned ritual?

Does the Blue Dot connect you to "pure potential" or hook you into the "unified field?"

Is the Blue Dot a rip-off? An insult to your intelligence? Is it embarrassing?

Is the Blue Dot stupid? Is it smart?

Is the Blue Dot a potential miracle-catalyst?

Is the Blue Dot whatever you want it to be?

Do you like the Blue Dot? Do you have one? Do you use it regularly?

My friend Annie notices the connection between finding pennies and experiencing good luck. Perhaps the penny reminds her to *experience* good luck, perhaps it is a *symbolic omen*, perhaps it is the Universe sending her a message. Maybe "selective attention" at work?

However it functions, Annie finds more pennies than anyone I know. We were once walking in the rain down a dark, bleak street in Lenox, Massachusetts, when she suddenly bent down and picked up a penny! It was so dark I couldn't see my shoes, but she found a penny.

Another time, Annie and I were walking through a modern art installation at the Massachusetts Museum of Contemporary Art. The floor of this rather large room was covered with thousands of sheets of paper. Every minute or so, one of a dozen little ceiling-mounted machines would drop another sheet of paper. That was the exhibit.

As we strolled through this mess of paper, I covertly took a penny out of my pocket and hid it in my palm. At a seemingly random moment, I bent down and pretended to find a penny under the mishmash of paper.

"Hey Annie, look ... I found a penny! Wow!"

Two seconds later (and I swear this is true) Annie kicks some of the paper, bends down and... "I found a dime," she said.

I replied, "How did you *do* that?"

Annie matter of factly said, "Well, you found a penny, so I was sure there was some more down there."

And no, she didn't palm it.

How do you think Annie came to find the dime? Was it an amazing coincidence?

Was it an example of a mind-altering synchronicity?

Did her subconscious mind create the dime out of subatomic particles?

Did Annie's non-conflicted "expectation" trigger of the result? What do *you* think happened?

Here are some easy-to-use mind-tools, attitude-tools and belief-tools that just might tip the good luck balance in your favor!

1. **Imagine yourself having good luck every day.** Get a clear picture of what good luck means to you, and visualize it. Daily.

2. **Desire the good luck.** Feel the emotional excitement and mental satisfaction. *Choose* to believe that you will have more good luck.

3. **Expect the good luck.** This is trainable, and it might take some discipline. Every day, remind yourself to expect the good luck. Even when things do not look like they are going your way, *still* find the lesson, remain optimistic, stay the course. Remember the yo-yo, and the recognition that what goes down could eventually (under the right conditions) come back up.

4. **Speak the language of good luck.** You can be in-between jobs instead of unemployed, or in-between relationships instead of single. Working in a restaurant, you can be an order-taker …or an experience-maker! When you label yourself, come up with forward-thinking, empowering, positive words that support the future you are creating.

5. **Network with lucky people.** This can be hit or miss, but network nonetheless—you never know who will be the key to your good luck! Be open-minded with people. Make follow-up phone calls and send thank you notes. Smile at people and make a little eye contact. Try expressing unconditional kindness as much as possible. Treat every customer as your "most valuable customer"… especially *yourself*!

6. **Write a gratitude journal every day.** Make a list of things, circumstances, conditions, relationships, etc., that you are truly grateful for. They can be tiny or huge, sacred or mundane, funny or serious, trivial or important—doesn't matter. Just list five things, and do it every day. Yes, you *can* repeat things. Do it any way you want—just do it.

7. **Carry a recording device.** Small digital voice recorders have come way down in price. Micro-cassette and cassette recorders are cheap. When you get a terrific idea, you can record it, so you'll remember it, and maybe even *take action*!

Jerry's Good Luck Affirmations

I experience my life as lucky.

I imagine, desire, and expect good luck.

I am allowed to have good luck.

I have permission for good luck.

I express gratitude for my good luck.

I interpret my life as one lucky moment after another.

I am the luckiest!

Good luck comes to me easily and effortlessly.

Good luck is a good thing!

My good luck blesses me, my family, friends, community, and planet.

I share my good luck with others.

I am happy to be lucky!

THE GOSPEL SINGER

"He who loses money, loses much; he who loses a friend, loses much more.
He who loses faith, loses all."
Eleanor Roosevelt

"Being cheerful keeps you healthy."
King Solomon

I recently had the pleasure of conducting a communications seminar for BerkshireWorks, an agency in Pittsfield that provides a range of social and vocational services.

As usual, I arrived forty-five minutes early, got my coffee and prepared the room. The first to arrive was Elizabeth, who told me that she worked at Goodwill and that Elder Services sent her.

The rest of the class arrived: a few middle-aged guys who lost their jobs due to layoffs, a young pregnant woman, an ambitious twenty-something dude with punk sensibilities, an ex-waitress social worker—about fifteen or sixteen in all.

I finished the show, and, as we were wrapping up and chatting, Elizabeth mentioned that she sang gospel.

"Alto?" I asked.

"Yes."

"Would you sing a little for us?"

"No, I couldn't."

"Oh, you sing in ensemble, only?"

"No, I sing some solo."

"Well, it would be quite a gift for us if you would sing a little."

"Well... okay."

She cleared her throat, apologized for being hoarse, and slowly began to sing a song about God and a sparrow. Her voice became more and more emotional and the technical quality—awesome! She completely and utterly blew us away. Eyes were getting misty. The perfectly controlled power and modulations in Elizabeth's voice were so unexpectedly virtuoso!

When she was finished, and the applause died down, I wanted to end the seminar by saying, "and *that* is an example of authentic communication." But I didn't need to say a word.

There was a lot of "information" in Elizabeth's segment of the program. Her first shy mention of her singing followed by her initial refusal to sing, the mind-blowing singing, the shameless expression of the deepest human emotions, the love and appreciation that came her way, the (I would have to say) "spiritual" experience that most all of the attendees seemed to share.

Do you have a special gift that you withhold? Do you need someone to talk you into singing that song, expressing that love, painting that picture, giving that speech, marketing your business?

Perhaps you can use Elizabeth's story to inspire you, or remind yourself, to express *more* of your confident, secure, creative, spiritual True Self ... in the areas of your of life that need it.

MAGICIAN'S CHOICE

"When a scientist states that something is possible, he is almost certainly right. When he states that something is impossible, he is very probably wrong."
  Arthur C. Clarke

"What if everything is an illusion and nothing exists? In that case, I definitely overpaid for my carpet."
  Woody Allen

Once upon a time, I was on a flight from Los Angeles to Boston, sitting next to a guy who looked like, well... Satan. He had the widow's peak, the pointy eyebrows. He turned out to be a well-known magical performer and mentalist.

We discussed projects and shoptalk for a while. Then he asked me, "Do you know about Magician's Choice?"

"Is this a trick question?" I asked.

"Magician's Choice," he intoned, "is very simple, yet very powerful. It is the magician *choosing* the outcome [of the magical working, trick or otherwise] in advance."

To demonstrate, he did a small performance with a flight attendant and headphones. The attendant was going down the aisle, asking passengers if they wanted to rent the headphones for the movie. I think it was four dollars. Down the aisle she went, handing out headphones and collecting money.

He said to me, "She'll offer you the headphones for $4.00 and she'll forget to ask me for the money and give me the headphones for free."

It was exactly as he predicted.

"Magician's Choice, Jerry. I chose the outcome in advance."

Interesting.

Did my magician friend influence her behavior with nonverbal communication, including his Satan-like appearance? Hypnotism? Did he project his thoughts, or an energy field of some kind, clogging the noggin of the attendant? Did the subatomic components of Magician's Choice alter the fabric of the time-space continuum?

Perhaps he had paid in advance. What do you think?

I think Magician's Choice has *plenty* of practical applications— magical and otherwise. To choose the outcome in advance sounds very smart to me!

To practice Magician's Choice, we must think in outcomes, goals, desired results. This means optimism! Certainty! Commitment!

Every successful act of "magic" I've observed seems to have produced outcomes that reverberate on material, mental, emotional and, (I'm taking an educated guess) spiritual levels as well. All of 'em! Therefore, we want to be careful what we wish for. These outcomes we're creating, first in our imagination, best be sharp, clear, non-conflicted, and bright. The daily focus of attention appears to be the key.

Where is the magic created? It could be created in the mind, the nervous system, the perceptions. It might be created by actions, behavior, communications.

It could be created by synchronicities, divine intervention, resonance. It might be created subatomically, energetically, metaphysically. What do you think?

The Inner World (unconscious drives, patterns, complexes) runs the Outer World (behavior, actions, reactions, responses), so don't neglect the inner world. Visualize your optimal future daily. Affirm your preferences for the future you're creating. Remind yourself, daily.

Is it simple? Of course it's simple.

Will it work? You know it!

So, what are we going to *do* about it?

TRANSFORMING THE "HOLIDAY BLUES"

"Life is an adventure in forgiveness."
Norman Cousins

"If you judge people, you have no time to love them."
Mother Teresa

We know holidays often contain emotional triggers. Christmas Eve, 1990. 11:00 PM. I was halfway to my Lenoxdale home from a holiday celebration in Richmond. Though I managed a smile on my face, I had a major case of the holiday blues and didn't even know it. That is, not until my car and I slid off the road into an icy ditch. I walked the two or three miles back to my friend's house in the rural, pre-cellphone, starry night of personal introspection, freezing my butt off and pondering why and how I caused this accident. In this case, there was no question in my mind. My unconscious, childhood-vintage holiday hurts-turned-into-angers squirted out in this very inconvenient form! The lesson: recognize, take ownership of, and "process" my feelings and hurts, before they "process" me!

Let's explore some holiday/birthday beliefs, thoughts, habits and patterns. Get some paper, a pen and some quality time to reflect.

First, write down elements of your *optimal* holiday/birthday experience. For this part of the exercise, you have no limits, no obligations, total flexibility. Anything goes. What would you do from mid-November to early January (or around birthday time) if you could do anything you wanted? What would happen? How would you feel? What gifts would you give and receive? How would you spend your time? What is important to you? What are your intentions?

Now, imagine you are a five or six-year-old child, and you can celebrate any way you'd like. Write down your Inner Child's picture of the best holiday season or birthday you can imagine, including important feelings like being loved, feeling secure, having enough, being good enough. Since this is taking place in your imagination, there are unlimited resources at your command. Don't hold back. While we're at it, we can create a mental movie where we, as a child, can actually *experience* that wonderful, loving, secure holiday/birthday. Remember, you have an unlimited expense account in your inner world, your imagination, your visualizations. Modern science suggests that the brain cannot differentiate between something vividly imagined and something that "actually" happened.

Take a break and ponder the meaning of that last sentence.

Back to the present. Make a list of obligations and tasks that your personal tradition (social, family, job-related, religious, cultural) says you *must do* for the holidays/birthday. Then, write out the feelings, good and bad, that are triggered by thoughts of these tasks and obligations. Be honest. This exercise is for you. We will not be collecting and grading your work! And by the way, spelling doesn't count, and neatness doesn't, either.

Now, an essay question: "What can I change this year to generate more good feelings and heal or eliminate a few of the problems?"

For example: If I continually feel disappointed because my holiday bonus is too small (or doesn't exist) and I need more approval from my boss, maybe *I can give myself* the approval I need and accept the fact that I project an approval-withholding "Daddy" onto my boss! If I feel like a martyr because I do too much cooking and entertaining, perhaps I can do a little less with no ill effect on my social standing. If I absolutely hate visiting certain people because I (and they) have a miserable time anyway, this year, how about a short, loving phone call instead? If I'm habituated to the "poor me" identity, perhaps I can change that to the "lucky me" or "new, improved me" identity! If I am addicted to complaining about my less-than-perfect past, I can "time travel" in my imagination, give myself a more empowering version, and spend that former complaint-time in more constructive and enjoyable pursuits.

We are now ready to set some specific goals for this holiday/birthday season. Write down the five most important things you need to do in order to make this holiday/birthday the best you've ever had. These goals may be health-related (eat less food, drink more water, exercise daily), mental (remember that I am responsible for my choices and decisions), emotional (I will care for and love myself more) and spiritual (I will consciously connect with my spiritual self at least once a day; I focus my attention on the spiritual aspects of the holiday, or of my own existence, for that matter). If applicable, jot down an action plan to turn those goals into solid realities.

If you are religious and believe in the power and efficacy of prayer ... then, for God's sake, pray about this! Daily, I suggest!

Positive affirmations are creative descriptions of the future we prefer. They are tools that direct our focus and attention toward our goals. Affirmations remind us what we want to be, have and create. Write some affirmations of your own, to support the achievement of each goal you set, and say them out loud at least ten times in the morning and ten times before bed. For example, if my goal is to have happier holidays, I might affirm: *I am understanding the nature of my own needs; I am graciously accepting all gifts of love; I am allowed to enjoy the holidays; I am making choices that result in happier holidays; I count my blessings; I have a wonderful life; I am grateful for the love that I have and the love that I can give.*

Our feelings are *so* powerful and have that funny way of materializing, even though we might want to hide them, deny them or minimize them. Better to be straight and honest with ourselves and make some positive decisions ... than habitually think the things and do the things that make us feel hurt, angry, and resentful year after year.

MOOD MANAGEMENT

"The problem is not that there are problems. The problem is expecting otherwise and thinking that having problems is a problem."
Theodore Rubin

"Half our fears are baseless; the other half discreditable."
Christian Bovee

"The only thing worse than watching a bad movie is being in one."
Elvis Presley

A woman was walking down the street when she heard what seemed like a soft, but firm, voice that said, "Don't take another step!" She stopped in her tracks, and a load of bricks fell from a construction site right in front of her. If she had kept walking, she would have been hit.

A few weeks later, she was driving down the New Jersey Turnpike and she heard the voice again. "Slow to 45, NOW!" She did, and saw a three-car collision happen right in front of her!

Then the voice spoke again. "I am your Guardian Angel and I am always here to protect you from disaster. Do you have anything you want to ask me?"

"Yes," she said. "Where were you on my wedding day?"

Isn't it amazing that one funny story—a huge jump (either way) in your stock portfolio, an unexpected act of extreme kindness, or a vivid, nostalgic childhood memory—can completely change your mood in a split second?

You can be worried about your job, angry about the traffic, or insecure about the future, when something happens and your emotional weather report shifts. Now, all of a sudden you're happy, and you've forgotten about the negative interpretations that were troubling you!

When astrologers study my natal chart and see the three planets in Cancer the Crab, the need for mood management is frequently mentioned, and accurately so. Over the years, I've learned to take an active approach to mood management instead of letting my past patterns do it (or not do it) for me. I came up with a checklist of sorts—things to consider and things to do—to assist me when a bad mood threatens to drain the joy and gratitude out of my nervous system. Try it!

1. Ask yourself, what was the mood trigger? Did you lie to yourself? Betray yourself? Did you say yes when you meant no, or no when you meant yes?

2. Are you telling yourself that you can't have something that you want? Why? Did *you* make yourself angry because you won't give yourself permission to have what you want?

3. Are you re-feeling familiar self-pity or self-condemnation feelings from your distant youth that have *nothing* to do with the present? Are you, in fact, older now? Do you, in fact, know better?

4. What were the words you used in the recent or distant past that made you feel powerless? Write some of them down:

_____

_____

_____

5. What are you telling yourself right now, this second? Write some of that down:

_____

_____

_____

6. Why do you think that you chose the negative opinion as your "absolute reality" instead of one of the more positive options? Do you realize that they are *just* opinions, notions, speculations, assumptions? Remember what assume means? Something about "making an ass out of you and me?"

7. Did you poison yourself with any of these statements: "I'll never be happy! No one understands me! Nobody loves me! What's the use? Nobody cares. I'm going to order a pizza, with pepperoni, and eat it all, and wash it down with beer. I'm going to smoke a cigarette. That movie, *It's a Wonderful Life*? That doesn't apply to me. Poor me! Poor, *poor me*! Woe is me! Woe, woe, woe!"

8. Find out what astrological sign the moon is transiting. Smile, and loudly exclaim, "Oh, so *that's* it!"

9. Breathe deeply for at least a few minutes. Don't stop.

10. Stay away from all activities that will make it worse.

11. Meditate on the future you would prefer.

12. Get out your journal and write about your feelings.

13. Read a book that will inspire you to become your powerful self again.

14. Read your personal mission statement out loud twice—three times, if necessary.

15. Play the "positive affirmation game" with yourself. Think only positive and constructive thoughts for five minutes. Then ten minutes. Then go for a half-hour. Try an hour.

16. Do some physical exercise, even if you don't want to.

17. Talk it out into a tape recorder for a few minutes, then listen to it.

18. Pray for assistance. Ask your Higher Self, Guardian Angels, Invisible Friends, and Cosmic Guides to give you the guidance and wisdom you need to get back to your joyful center. Then, accept the assistance.

19. Write down twenty things, circumstances, relationships, items, situations and/or experiences you are truly and deeply grateful for.

20. Have a double espresso.

21. Watch an episode of *Seinfeld*.

WHEN BUSINESS IS SLOW ... WRITE YOUR BOOK

"In the mind there are no limits."
Dr. John Lilly

"Fears are educated into us, and we can if we choose, get them educated out."
Karl Menninger

"I feel good!"
James Brown

"What—me worry?"
Alfred E. Newman

I was addicted to worry. My custom designed crap-trigger was often activated by some expense—personal, business-related, $40.00 or $4000.00—it didn't matter. Printing a new brochure, buying a new suit, a guitar, software—I'd spend the money and then worry about it. I wonder, wonder, wonder where that worry might have come from?

Once in a while I'd worry about my health or my career, the state of the planet, relationships. Usually expenses. Not money. Expenses. The worry fed my insecurities. The insecurities fed the worry. Nice! Very attractive!

In 1999, I wrote:

I write these words from a committed standpoint—committed to continual improvement. I want to better my life in every way. I want more emotional mastery, more productivity, better moods for longer duration, increased wealth, a successful business and loving relationships. I want to be happier and more grateful. And that is why I teach it!

WHEN BUSINESS IS SLOW ... WRITE YOUR BOOK is one of my working titles for the book that is to be written sometime in my future. I don't know when it will be written ... but I do know it will be!

Other working titles:

I TOOK MY OWN ADVICE ... AND IT WORKED!
POSNER'S POSITIVE PATH
THE POSITIVE DIARIES
DIARY OF A POSITIVE GUY
ONE MAN'S POSITIVE PATH
POSNER'S POSITIVE PATHWORK
POSNER'S POSITIVE PATHWORK DIARY
WALKING THE POSITIVE PATH WITH POSNER
MY POSITIVE PATH
MY LIFE AS A BELIEF EXPLORER
POSNER'S EXPERIMENTS IN BELIEF
BELIEF SYSTEM WORKOUT
PRISONER OF POSITIVITY
IT WORKED FOR ME
THE BEST ADVICE FOR OPRAH WATCHERS AND SELF-HELP AFICIONADOS

Note to Self: When things are not going as I think they should, *do something constructive*! Be creative. Cease the *kvetching*! Move the energy and move the body! As George Costanza learned in one especially productive episode of *Seinfeld*, try doing the opposite of your usual behavior.

My New Year's resolution for 1999 is to cease unnecessary worrying. Worrying does not make me powerful, successful, happy, strong, rich, or good-looking. Worrying does not solve the problem or get the job done. Worrying sucks!

I have choices. I can worry about the money. I can have hope. I can see the expense as an investment and expect that my investment will have a positive return in some form. I can freak out. I can see the positive potential. I can be the adult. I can enjoy the possibilities. I can give up and die. I can eat cheesecake. I can write a book about it. I can shape my destiny.

Every moment I have *so* many options and choices. My future is, at the very least, *influenced* by my choices—choices of thought, feeling, belief, and action. I am in the driver's seat. I can choose consciously and wisely *only* when I know the outcomes I prefer.

And what about those negative addictions? Am I, in fact, chemically addicted to the hormones released by bad moods or bad feelings? Let's see. Fill in the blanks:

My most obvious negative addiction is to:_____

_____

I love this addiction because: _____

_____

Today, my conscious choice is to: ____ keep it ____ lose it.

My secret negative addiction is to: _____

_____

I love this addiction because: _____

_____

Today, my conscious choice is to: ____ keep it ____ lose it

I can't change what I don't notice. I desire more awareness of my limiting, negative and simply *wrong* habits and patterns that are running me. I ask myself, "Where the hell did *those* come from?"

WRONG = COUNTERPRODUCTIVE

Some of my WRONG relationship habits/patterns/beliefs/opinions:

_____

_____

_____

_____

Some of my WRONG work habits/patterns/beliefs/opinions:

_____

_____

_____

_____

Some of my WRONG communication habits/patterns/beliefs/opinions:

_____

_____

_____

_____

Some of my WRONG lifestyle habits/patterns/beliefs/opinions:

_____

_____

_____

_____

Now ... write yourself some "reality checks" and hope they won't bounce! Put a check mark next to the "realities" you like the most.

____ I am an extremely fortunate person.

____ I make my choices based on the outcomes I most desire

____ I am grateful for my life now. I love my life now.

____ I am happy, healthy, and living my dream.

____ My net worth and my self-worth increases every day.

____ I consciously (and with a positive spin, I might add) manage my: moods, love, service, fun, money, romance, career, identity, communications, family, playtime, work time, relationships, group activities, spiritual practice, learning, philosophy, higher consciousness pursuits.

____ I do a lot of good.

____ I have a lot of fun.

____ I can change my life for the better, *now!*

Note from the present: Now, worry is conspicuous by its absence!

20 SHORT SUGGESTIONS, REMINDERS, AND ADVICE-BLIPS

"Be like a postage stamp. Stick to it until you get there."
Harvey Mackay

"Decide what's right before you decide what's possible."
Brian Tracy

"Take a broom and clean someone's house. That says enough."
Mother Theresa

Sometimes we want to reach a little higher, feel a little better, accomplish a little more, act a little smarter! Sometimes, a small reminder will trigger the state of awareness that catalyzes the improvement. By using the "magic repetition factor"—daily—we can condition/train/program ourselves to make the improvements automatically, spontaneously, and on an ongoing basis. Small keys can open the largest doors!

1. Stack the odds in your favor… express unconditional kindness to yourself and others.
2. Look fear in the eye and say, "I'm making you up in my head!"
3. Resolve the conflicts about your own desires and just watch the miracles happen!
4. Use your conflict resolution skills to mediate YOUR OWN inner conflicts.
5. Research, then rehearse, the outcomes you most desire.
6. Ask the right people for help ... not the wrong people.
7. Invest energy developing your passion.
8. Don't dumb down, smarten up.
9. The right people are headed your way. Recognize them.

10. Stop engineering your own frustrations.
11. Create a Whine-Free Zone.
12. Be your own American Idol.
13. Practice "Intelligent Optimism!"
14. Remember, failure is not an option—it is an interpretation.
15. Know the myths that drive your behavior.
16. You can learn something from everything and anything. So take notes.
17. Don't quit five minutes before the miracle is scheduled to happen.
18. Ask yourself, "How much time and energy do I waste trying to maintain my illusion of control?"
19. If you must do "what-ifs"—make them positive!
20. Remember, it is the giver that reaps the best rewards.

THE POSITIVE RAP

Friends of mine.
Precious cargo.
Freedom to lift
emotional embargos.

Giver.
Receiver.
Taker.
Faker.
Believer.
Transceiver.
Transcender.
Positive blender.
Positive Times-er
Emotion refiner.

List your triggers.
List your buttons.
Have some lobster,
Try the mutton.
Where is the charge
on the ego barge?
Cutting your losses
From the negative bosses.

A mighty guitar chord can change the vibrations.
A change of perspective could trigger elation!

Gurus I have known ...
and the seeds they had sown...
grew into roses nonetheless!

Some ideas I've entertained ...
and some habits that I'd trained ...
at times would seem to drain me!
But the daily positive work ...
kept me from feeling like a jerk ...
and rescued me from murky thinking!

THE NOWSELF AND THE FUTURESELF

The Nowself and the Futureself are meeting in your head.
The Nowself and the Futureself are moving your life ahead.
The Nowself and the Futureself, creating your very next move.
The Nowself and the Futureself are in the cosmic groove!
The Nowself and the Futureself are dreaming up some fun!
The Nowself and the Futureself—their positive magic is never done!
From the future P.O.V.—"it already happened to me!"

And if you must judge, judge the inner judge!
Ask God Almighty to give you a friendly nudge!
If you must indulge, then eat the fudge!
If you want to be free, then release the grudge!
For the good of all and with harm to none,
So it is written, so it is done!

IRREFUTABLE PROOF OF THE EXISTENCE OF GOD

Look in a mirror.

ESTEEM-BOOSTING WORDS FOR FUN AND PROFIT

I am decisive.
I aim at the target.
I am powerful.
I am successful.
I am focused on the important outcomes.
I am a powerful choice-maker.
I choose practical and fun interpretations.
I honor my personal and professional cycles.
I allow more professional success.
I have permission for positive impact with greater ease.
I am a person with a mission.
I am allowed to be creative and productive
I am allowed to be happy, healthy, wealthy and wise.
I give love and respect
I am loved and respected.
I choose positive, empowering assumptions and notions.
I self-suggest positive realities.
I get all of my work done with ease.
I have virtually unlimited resources.
I choose positive, expansive, helpful, joyous possibilities.

VERY BAD IDEAS

Self-pity.
Negative assumptions.
Baseless fears.
Making mountains out of molehills.
Chronic *kvetching*.
Procrastination.
Irrational thinking.
Too much *halvah*.

NEW BEGINNINGS OPERA THEATRE

[Ed. Note: Stay with this—it's a trip!]

Libretto

The turning of the cycles is nigh. Characters, in anticipation of another excellent year, crowd around a giant, holographic calendar and dance like there's no tomorrow to the music of the future.

Pooped, they sit around in a circle, some beating small drums, a few playing poker, two or three couples intensely engaged in conversation. An attractive middle-aged man, smoking Balkan Sobranie tobacco in a meerschaum pipe shaped like Frank Zappa's head, sits in an uncomfortable looking yoga pose.

A clock strikes the midnight hour. The crowd becomes silent. Then Mr. Mubuto steps into the spotlight and sings...

Mr. Mubuto

The final day of this cycle was the day to cease the worrying.
The worrying is a habit and I know it.
Ghosts. Phantoms. Fade them out, with the fader.
Give them their walking papers!
I want to be sure of my choices as I mute their voices.

Lester

Running barefoot in the quantum field,
we speak our own language, and observe the yield.

Mrs. Attanasio

And now, a word from our sponsor ...

Announcer

Infect *your* business with Posner's Positive Idea Viruses.

You will love it … and so will your customers!

Celestial Choir
I can break any habit, I can make any habit.

Magician, Metaphysician, Mystic, and Miracle Maker
(in four-part Beach Boys-style harmony)

We are creating more joy.
We reinvent our lives.

I have faith.
I love.
I am improving.
I am doubt-removing.

I am the magician.
I am the metaphysician.
I am the mystic.
I am the miracle maker.
Yeah! Yeah! Yeah!!

Announcer
Yes, faith, love, focus, and commitment assist you in achieving your goals … now, better than ever!

(the scene shifts to a classroom)

Pablo
This class is for people who have a strong desire for positive change and growth. Okay? Okay! Class, repeat after me, please …

I make up Sandra stories, I make up Peggy stories.
(I make up Sandra stories, I make up Peggy stories.)
I make up Jim and Jack, Vickie and Mubuto stories.
(I make up Jim and Jack, Vickie and Mubuto stories)

ATTENTION LATE BLOOMERS: YOU'RE RIGHT ON TIME!

I make up work stories, I make up money stories.
(I make up work stories, I make up money stories.)
I make up client stories, I make up vendor stories.
(I make up client stories, I make up vendor stories.)
I make up emotional stories, I make up spiritually uplifting stories.
(I make up emotional stories, I make up spiritually uplifting stories.)
I continually revise these stories.
(I continually revise these stories.)

Pablo

Very good!

Class

Very good!

Pablo

Okay, you can stop now.

Class

Okay, you can stop now.

Suki

The miracles I want to make are often miracles of understanding.
Teaching myself to raise my own self-esteem with thoughts, words and deeds.

Pablo

Promoting good ideas. Good words and good deeds. Good idea!
Creating and maintaining positive relationships every moment.

Suki

Intention is everything. Know your intention.

Celestial Choir

Release the hyper-positive "idea-virus" now!

The Happy Salesman
I've got new revelations for human relations!

Choir and Entire Cast
With *awesome* positive results!

Magician
I am the magician.
Metaphysician
I am the metaphysician.
Mystic
I am the mystic.
Miracle Maker
I am the miracle maker.

Choir and Entire Cast
Yeah! Yeah! Yes! Yeppers! Da! Si! Oui! Kain! Ja! Yessiree!

CURTAIN

THE AUTHENTIC SMILE

"I have the world's largest collection of seashells. I keep it on beaches all over the world."
   Steven Wright

A frog went to see a psychic. "I see you meeting a smart, beautiful woman who will be very interested in you ... she'll want to know everything about you." "That's great," said the frog, "where will I meet her?" "Biology class."

The palm reader read both my hands and said they contradicted each other. "So which should I believe?" I asked. "Definitely the first," the palmist said. "You should never trust second hand information!"

Start by remembering three things in your life—circumstances, relationships, possessions, activities—that make you smile:

1._____
2._____
3._____

The "authentic smile" is a wonderful indicator, as well as creator, of *so* many positive conditions—happiness, appreciation, gratitude, joy, good vibes, and fun, for example. Does the authentic smile operate as an endorphin trigger, making happiness bigger, producing vim and vigor? What can increasing the authentic smile frequency do for me? Make me feel better? Improve business? Contribute to the positive evolution of my relationships? Reduce stress? Show me that I can condition my own responses?

In 1992, as I began free-lancing and developing a career as a speaker, I noticed that, whenever the phone rang, my heart would beat a little faster and I'd experience the sensation of stress hormones rushing into my body and my mind. For various reasons, I had associated the phone ringing with bad news instead of good news, and that this association with negative results operated automatically.

As an experiment, I wrote down the following words: Whenever the phone rings, I smile. I read the words daily. I kept reading the words. Daily. Then, I started smiling more. Especially when the phone rang. Arf! Arf! Bow-wow! Woof! Just call me Pavlov Posner!

Waiters, bartenders, cashiers, telephone operators, salespeople are compelled to smile. Friends exchange smiles as signs of acceptance, comfort, fun, and love. The authentic smile sends one message, the frown sends another.

Here's a question: does smiling more in a work context (for example— smiles by choice, or smiles by company protocol) create benefits that spill over to other areas of life as well?

Is smiling more something worth experimenting with? Is smiling more a way to generate more positive self-fulfilling prophesies? Will smiling more help me cope? Make me more successful?

Do you want to smile more? Yes? Then, here are some suggestions to consider.

1. Remind yourself to smile more. Write it on your to-do list. Make little cards. Put a small sign by your bathroom mirror. Write yourself some smile affirmations like:
    I like to smile more.
    I am allowed to smile more.
    I have permission to smile more.
    I see the value in smiling more.
    I remember to smile more.
    SMILE = SUCCESS
    I am spreading more good vibes with my authentic smile.
2. Once a day, take a "smile meditation." Sit down and close your eyes, and relax (not while you're driving, please). Imagine yourself in a situation that makes you smile. Visualize the scene as vividly and clearly as you can. As you're doing this, enjoy the sensations and smile. Two or three minutes a day.
3. Get the long-awaited Brian Wilson album, SMiLE. Listen to it, using the cover and box as yet another "smile-reminder."

4. Remember comedy albums? Most of the ones you loved as a kid are available now on CD. Get a few of your favorites, and play them in the car. I worked at all-comedy KMDY radio in the mid-80s, and as I drove down Thousand Oaks Boulevard, I'd see people driving in their cars... laughing hysterically... listening to our station! Imagine sitting at a red light, and in the car next to you, is a person laughing hysterically. Well, that person can be you! The very funny *Prairie Home Companion* joke shows from NPR are available on cassette and CD. Get them and play them in the car.

5. Make a list of things that make you smile. You might even consider writing a "smile journal" or a "smile supplement" to your daily gratitude journal. Work on the list. Edit the list. Put your attention on the list daily.

6. Learn one *really* good all-purpose joke. Practice it until you feel confident enough to tell it. Tell it, observe the response, don't get discouraged, and practice some more!

7. Whether you're pondering deep philosophical conundrums, praying, meditating, communing with the spiritual world, eating a turkey sandwich, or shopping for socks, feel the gratitude, have the fun, dig on the cosmic coolness of it all... and smile.

MEET YOUR NERVOUS SYSTEM

"We all have many more abilities and internal resources than
we know.
My advice is that you don't need to break your neck to find out
about them."
Christopher Reeve

"Try not. Do, or do not. There is no try."
Yoda, the Jedi Master

Is it possible... that we receive more than a billion signals from the
environment every minute, but we're only aware of one or two of
them at any given moment?

Information pours in, and our nervous system sorts it out, making
evaluations, bringing to our attention what we "think" is important, and
pretty much ignoring the rest.

At the same time, "brain circuits" or "instincts" or "survival
programs" are running below our threshold of awareness, keeping us safe
from danger, and keeping us alive!

When you drive down a busy road, for example, do you notice all of
the street signs? The sound of your car's engine? The makes and models
of all of the other cars? The humidity? The stores that you drive by? And
who, exactly, *is* the driver of the car? Are you driving, or are your "habits"
driving the car?

Speaking to a friend, do you notice the pitch and modulation of the
voice, the facial expressions, the sounds of other people walking by, the
copy machine, the radio in the background, the hum of the fan, the color
of the floor, the feel of the chair, the beating of your heart?

How much do we notice, and why do we notice what we do?

I think one of the great, elementary life-truths is that you can't
change what you don't notice.

By regularly directing our own attention to those areas we wish to change or improve, might we increase the likelihood that we'll actually *do something* about it?

Can we make alliances with our own nervous system? For example, what do you think could happen if you read the following paragraph once a day, and think about it for a minute or two?

I create my future, or at least influence my future, with my beliefs, thoughts and habits; with my communications and expectations; with my desire, intention, and attention; and with my behaviors and my actions.

After a month or two of this exercise, do you think you'd notice your beliefs more? Become more aware of your thoughts and habits? More conscious of how you communicate... and what you expect? Could this make a difference in your life?

I'd say so!

And now, let's travel in our imaginations to New York's fabulous and colorful Greenwich Village for a performance of...

THE POSITIVE PESSIMIST
An Opera

ACT ONE

We are in the year 2012. The set is decorated with a mix of 1940s, 50s, 60s, 70s, 80s, 90s and contemporary styles. A real mishmash, but somehow it works. Some characters are wearing vintage costumes, some in future fashions. The cast of seven men and seven women stroll in from both sides of the stage, in a festive mood. A few cast members climb up the front of the stage, everyone dances around a little, some shaking their booty, others waltzing. They slowly gather around the announcer ...

Announcer
This performance of The Positive Pessimist is made possible by a grant from The Posner Group—(harp glissando), where the philosophical speculations are practical, and classical positive thinking is promoted!

The Seeker
I am the King of Choice,
with a helping hand and heart.
Extending healing. Positive feeling.
Having fun. Consciously managing, navigating!
Secure and safe in the arms of my Queen,
I guided my kingdom into the positive future.

I have my mission, I have no woes.
I have my direction, I have my magic list of goals!

Chorus
The magic list of goals. (harp glissando)

Mrs. Attanasio
Always remember your goals!

I say, never forget your goals!
A goal is attention. A goal needs retention.
A goal requires understanding. A goal can be demanding.
A goal can be great. A goal can be healing.
A goal can be accomplishment. A goal can be a feeling.
And ya can't hit the bull's eye if you can't see the target!

Parsifal
What do I get ... and ... what can I give?
The giver of the gift benefits most, you know.
It is the giver who should be thankful!

Celestial Choir
Who will reshape your motivations?
Who will mold you into your future-self?
And... *oh*, the diversity!

Pookie
Frank Zappa, Ghetto Rappers,
Monty Hall, Lauren Bacall,
Mother Love, boxing gloves,
Arthur Lee, the bumble bee,
Morris the Cat, Devo hats,
Soupy Sales, ten penny nails, boats with sails,
stores with holiday sales, supermarkets, and superstring theories.

(spoken) And somehow, somewhere, some time... The Creator...
created... me!

Entire Cast
We used to be pessimistic
No way were we altruistic!
The glass was empty, and the thinking was faulty,
The asses were dancing, and the egos were prancing
Down the gangplank to the ego barge.

Farewell negative ego,
Sail away on the ego barge.

Sail away, farewell.
Sail away, farewell ...

We choose optimism now!

ACT TWO

Mr. P. and Chorus

We have good luck!
Our luck continues due to factors known and unknown.
(yes, it does)!
Some stuff I control, and some I don't.
(yeah, yeah, yeah)!
But we get luckier and luckier the more we "do the Inner Work!"
Yes, we get luckier and luckier the more we "do the Inner Work!"

Play to win and win to play. Focus on the target each and every
day!
... aiming at the 'ol bull's eye!

Announcer

No actual bull was harmed in the writing of this opera.

Celestial Choir

THE POWER TO SEE MIRACLES.
THE POWER TO CREATE MIRACLES.
Positive change ... managing change ...
Make a miracle today!
Because we want to, we want to,
We want to make those miracles, we want to!

Pookie

Hey buddy ... ya need wisdom?

Mr. P.

Oh, yes, wisdom. I want that, too.
I wanna be wise, I wanna be true,

I wanna be good, skip-to-my-Lou,
I am calling yooooo-oooohhh-eeeee-ooooooo!

The Seeker

Who will answer? Who will answer?
The Inner Self? The Higher Self? Ed Ames?
My mojo's working magic, my love is on the line.
The message on the sign says it's introspection time!

Values transforming again and again.

People's stories float down my stream.
The coffee is delicious, as I live my dream.
All about survival, and the choices.
All about success, and the Rolls Royces.
All about the Truth, and a customized religion.
All about service, and the most sacred missions.

Some habits do break by themselves, so to speak.
We outgrow them.
And some just keep popping up again and again.
We get to know them.

Pookie and Mr. P.

Look! It's the Crab Man!

The Crab Man

I'm a Crab Man in the crab lands,
My shell is breaking and I'm stuck in the sand.
Another guy come over with a little green book,
A pail and shovel and sifter he brought,
And I, the Crab Man, gave him such a look!
Crab Man!
Yes, I'm the Crab Man
CRAB MAN!!!!!

Celestial Choir

Come out of your shell!

The Seeker

Give faith another chance!

Celestial Choir

Pessimism will not help you!

Pookie and Mr. P.

We're proposing positive resonance in all worlds,
activating mental magic to create the wealth and security we want.
Behaving MORE RESPONSIVELY and less reactively.

The Seeker

(spoken) Give yourself permission to change your life for the better. Imagine the improvements, daily. Focus your desire, and amp up anticipation. Ask the right people for help.

Celestial Choir

Permission, permission, permission. Daily ... daily ... daily! Ohhh Kaaay!

The End

POSITIVE PROGRAMMING PHRASES TO PONDER

"If I believe I cannot do something, it makes me incapable of doing it. But when I believe I can, then I acquire the ability to do it, even if I did not have the ability in the beginning."
   Mahatma Gandhi

I practice nonattachment.
I consciously catalyze positive changes in my life and work.
Nonetheless, I practice nonattachment and go with the flow.

I have become "the future self" of my past.
I practice non-attachment as appropriate.

I am currently creating "the future self" of my future.
I move my projects forward.
I select a state of continual growth and learning.
Still, I practice nonattachment.

The happiness level continues to rise.
The access to resources increases.
I am fulfilling my lifelong ambition -- to grow up!
I invoke the Great Divine Invisible Emotional Repair Corps.

Just the same, I practice nonattachment!

THE POSITIVE AFFIRMATION NEWSGROUP

Subject: Affirmations, Money and Otherwise
From: FuturaChick (Juanita Palabra)

Hola!

Need dinero? I am having mucho success using the following positive word formulas, which focus my attention on the money issues I desire to resolve. I meditate on them daily.

My Money Affirmations:
I am updating my money beliefs.
I choose to be secure about money.
I have enough money, which I can spend any way I want.
My money grows and grows and grows and grows.
I make more and more and more money.
I expand my success.
I feel safe, secure and loved.
My value increases.
Every day in every way I get better and better.
I deliver the goods.
I bring home the bacon.
I make BLTs.
Yummy!

Does the act of burning positive affirmations into the nervous system *really* create reality? I say, YES!

And, when I do visit the "emotional poopie bin," these are the questions I've remembered to ask myself:

What, exactly, am I "getting" from this drama?
What, exactly, am I "getting" from this worry?
What, exactly, am I "getting" from these bad feelings?

What, exactly, am I "getting" from this experience?
What, exactly, am I "getting" from this perspective?

Expanding the cube, always,
FuturaChick

Subject: Look at the Big Picture
From: Meetball (Al Bondegas)

People measure riches and success in thousands of ways. I look at it this way, if I'm alive ... I'm "up" for the day ...WAY up!
"If you don't think every day is a great day try going without one."

Optimistically yours,
Meetball

Subject: BoodaStuff
From: MrsAttanasio (Mary Attanasio)

I heard this story: Once a student of Buddhism told the Roshi that he thought he was nearing enlightenment, because during meditation he had a clear vision of the Buddha. His teacher frowned and asked, "If you go to sleep tonight and dream that you have won the lottery, do you wake up any richer?"
But ... maybe you *do* wake up richer! Maybe more hopeful? More positive? Happier? Maybe the student *was* nearing enlightenment! Maybe the *teacher* was having a crappy day!

Love,
Mary

Subject: Choice or habit?
From: Coogerman (Dr. Glenne Coogerman)

Have you ever gotten mad at yourself for making, what you defined as a Bad Decision? Then you beat up on yourself because you expected yourself to act on knowledge that you either forgot ... or never learned in the first place? And then ... the so-called bad decision began a chain reaction that resulted in the miracle?

Was the "getting mad at yourself" a choice ... or a habit?

Habit awareness is a *huge* key to positive change.

And when the going gets rough, *accelerate* your pathwork. Challenges are a call for processing and programming. When adversity strikes - that's when the learning gets deeper.

Current life events show me what I've learned ... and what might need some positive attention.

The mistake I made (or thought I made) might not be as important as the insight received ... and the actions I take now!

Playing my part in the drama of life unfolding,
Coogerman

JOURNALS I HAVE WRITTEN... AND LOVED

Daily journal writing is a great tool for personal growth and increased self-awareness. Just look at the cost/benefit ratio. Writing your thoughts in a daily journal can assist the healing process and promote learning, both of which might improve productivity and organization. And it gives amazing perspectives on your past.

Yes, there is nothing quite like going back to something written ten or fifteen years ago and seeing that information from the point of view of what was then your future-self!

This book you're reading now is a kind of journal—a journal of reminders, observations, tools, techniques, positive triggers ...

I learned early on that the more I focus on positive stuff, the more positive I become. And, after years of philosophical struggle, I had eventually **accepted as a basic value**: positive is better!

In 1990, after publishing the premiere issue (pamphlet) of *The Posnerian Times*, the name was changed to the slightly more commercial sounding: *The Positive Times*. My intention was to share my path of healing and optimism in a newsletter or magazine format. I also wanted to discipline myself to be more positive and heal my own hurts and I thought that writing a magazine about it would help. It did.

If *you* want to become more positive or heal your own hurts and turbo-charge your own growth and awareness process, I suggest that you begin (or continue) the form of journaling that you like the most.

Here are some examples:

1. **The Diary Journal.** Write down things that happened to you, things you did, activities, emotions you experienced, insights you gained. This is a free-form journal. Write what you want to ... whenever you want to! Having a problem, or a great success? Write about it!
2. **The Gratitude Journal.** As a behavior/attitude/perception modification tool, this one really must be practiced daily.

Once a day, every day, write down five things, circumstances, people, blessings, miracles, gifts, et cetera, that you are truly and deeply grateful for. For example: I'm grateful for my good health. I'm grateful for running hot water in my shower. I'm grateful for clearance sales. I'm grateful for my friends, my family, my computer, my endocrine system... The Beatles, Mozart, Seinfeld, Einstein, Leslie Gore... I'm grateful my stocks went up, I'm grateful I have stocks ... I'm grateful that I live in the Berkshires, I'm just grateful I'm alive! Just five a day—but *every day*. Write your gratitude journal on a pad, in a book, or on your computer—doing it in your head doesn't have the same impact. When you experiment with the gratitude journal, you can expect to feel more grateful, behave in a more grateful way, probably have less stress and—the bonus—you'll show yourself how, using repetition and focus, you can change some of your own mental, emotional, perceptual, and behavioral habits. Cool! And if you're having a challenging day, *read* your gratitude journal and you just might snap yourself out of an undesirable mood.

3. **The Audio Journal.** Get a small digital voice recorder or micro-cassette recorder. When you are inspired, when you get a brilliant idea, when you need to vent, record it. When you want insights, listen to it. If you sing or play a musical instrument, regularly record your stuff—polished or improvised, it doesn't matter. Just do it.

4. **The Smile Journal.** Write down five things a day that make you smile. Jokes, stories, ideas, perspectives, observations, hopes, dreams, kind acts, music, art. Five things ... daily.

5. **The Anger Journal.** When you're angry or annoyed (insecure or hurt), write about it. Go back from time to time and see what your anger triggers *used* to be!

6. **The Scrapbook Journal.** Cut and paste articles, pictures, quotations, your own writings, cartoons, doodles, into your scrapbook. Do it *your* way!

7. **The Stream of Consciousness Journal.** Just write. Anything. No censorship or editing.

8. **Your Journal as Your Book.** Take any form of journal writing that you've done and edit it for publication.

9. **The Affirmation Journal.** Write about your life in a series of positive affirmations. Affirm the good that you've already created, and write the affirmations that will create the mental/emotional/spiritual bridge to your optimal future.

Create the life you've always wanted to live. Frame the world the way you want it to be. A positive attitude is irresistible. Try one!

AFFIRMATIONS TO SUPPORT POSITIVE CHANGES

An affirmation is a statement of being—a statement of your own beliefs about yourself and your world. By consciously repeating positive statements, the mind eventually accepts them, and arranges perceptions to support and "create reality" consistent with the positive statement.

If you can also visualize and *feel* the affirmation, your results could come quickly. If you can use your imagination to cause fear and anxiety, why not use your imagination to cause success and happiness? [Good question. Ed.]

Today I am a new person.
I am new and improved.
I feel great about myself.
I am moving forward to a wonderful future.
The universe supports my positive changes.
I am secure and confident in my ability to let go
of the old habits, paradigms, illusions.
I am nurturing my own growth.
I am letting it be "different" this time.
I am facing a wonderful future.
I rejoice in every adventure.
I can become whatever I want to become.

Check the ones that apply. Use pencil. Review often. Read 'em aloud!

____ I absolutely deserve success.
____ I am really, really grateful.
____ My life is better now than it ever was.
____ My thoughts create my reality.

___ My feelings create my reality.

___ I choose to accept love.

___ I practice daily.

___ My spiritual work is really important.

___ I am ready to finally, really succeed.

___ I agree that happiness can be achieved.

___ My creative energy is at an all time high.

___ I believe I can, therefore I can.

___ My happiness is in harmony with universal law.

Career Guidance Department

If you already adore your work, turn the page. If not, vividly imagine what sort of work you would really, really enjoy doing. See yourself earning the kind of money that will make you happy. Say out loud, "I, (your name), am taking positive steps forward so I can have a happy, prosperous, healthy life. I am seeing opportunities for my growth!"

We spend *so* much of our time working that it pays to examine our attitudes about work. How come some people are able to do what they are happy doing, and others feel they are trapped in a miserable job with no way out? Could it be programming from childhood that work has to be painful? Could it be such a need for approval that we would perform a job we hate in exchange for a few pats on the back and a paycheck? Maybe we just don't believe we deserve to have a wonderful time working.

But w*ork can be fun* (despite what we might have been taught). Whatever your situation, whatever your mindset, no matter how old or young you are, you can change a bad situation into a terrific situation!

Say these work affirmations aloud, especially on Mondays!

I am getting joy out of my work.
I am calm and powerful in the workplace.
I am consciously feeling joy as I work.
I imagine myself doing exactly the kind of job I want to do.
I am projecting enthusiasm through my work.
I am upgrading my concept of work.
I am associating fun and love with work.
I can give myself as much approval as I need.
I am doing better every day.
I am accepting the possibility that I can have fun working.
My self-confidence expands at work.

A big key: Define your life's purpose and choose work that supports it. *It is never too late to change!*

It is also never too late to smile, laugh, be happy, be positive, accept love, be conscious, forgive freely, expect the best, relax, allow yourself to heal, create new and better realities, give yourself positive input, upgrade your belief systems, accept the gifts, get high on your life, break old and destructive habits, create lots of success, empower yourself, boost your own self-esteem, start a new life every day, enjoy the possibilities, tell yourself good things, stop hurting yourself, heal, and love your own inner child.

ON THE PATH WITH HELENE JONES

by Howie Doohan [One of Jerry's hipster subpersonalities. Ed.]

Helene Jones was feeling the lowdown. Despite her obvious cognitive mastery and butt-kicking victory at Old Man Gluberman's Poetry Slam recently, the auto-pessimism kicked in again—full force this time. *Que lastima*! *Oy vey*! Her buttons got pushed by most anyone that day, one right after another.

I made the scene to her pad to shoot the breeze, and for Annie's Fine Biscotti with chai tea.

Helene was straight from the fridge! Like, totally cool. She told me that she remembered how to disconnect the buttons using Posner's SNIP (Stop Negativity I Perceive) technique and, for the first time in recent history, soundly defeated her negative cogitating. We rapped about miracles and positive thinking until the wee hours of the AM. I hit the road around six.

I picked up a java-to-go at Bishoff's, negotiated my way to the bus stop, sat down on the bench, and began my wait for the 168 bus from Teaneck, New Jersey to the Port Authority Terminal, 42nd Street. I was thinking about Helene's unique Path, and my own optimal futures ... and breakfast muffins ... when I saw a small fleet of Mercedes Limos, each with a bumper sticker that seemed to speak to the very core of my being! Was this simply a coincidence? Or was it quantum physics at work? Maybe I just imagined it. Might this be The Sign I've been waiting for?

And here they are ... Howie Doohan's Bumper Stickers Of Destiny!

DON'T QUIT FIVE MINUTES BEFORE THE MIRACLE HAPPENS.

MONEY ISN'T EVERYTHING... BUT IT MIGHT BE SOMETHING!

I want us BOTH to win.

WRONG THINKING COULD BE THE ENEMY!

MOTHER, FATHER, SIBLING, SELF ...
All human, all forgiven.

Experiment with UNCONDITIONAL KINDNESS.

Honk if you're Master of Your Domain!

The last limo drove off down Cedar Lane. I now had a mild case of
"synchronicity ecstasy." My bus came; I sat down and started to write ...
The roles we play in life might be observed as a series of theatre games.
We play the roles we have become comfortable playing. We're appearing
as actors, often acting ancient roles, somehow managing to forget that
we are on stage. Wasn't it the French stage magician Robert-Houdin who
said, "A magician is an actor playing the part of a magician?"
The bus stopped, I got off, and a hippie girl wearing Birkenstocks
(and socks) handed me this flyer:

The POSICRUCIANS (not a religious organization)
INVITE YOU TO PONDER THE FOLLOWING IDEA-
VIRUSES:

Win the war against PERFECTIONISM, INSECURITY and
LEARNED HELPLESSNESS!

WHAT'S MY NEXT MAGNIFICENT OBSESSION?

How, exactly, have I been fooling myself lately?

Work works!

Help! I'm a PRISONER OF POSITIVITY!

Where Did I Graduate and Where Am I Still in School?

Oh the fearful and guilt-provoking things we make up in our heads!

SMILE. LAUGH. MAKE EYE CONTACT.

When my expectations are irrational,
I might get irrational results.
But then again, maybe not!

My needs are met ... how about yours?

Take Care of ALL the Inner Children!

Just Because You THINK Words In Your HEAD ...
Doesn't Mean That They're True.

MOVING TOO FAST TO BE KIND?—Slow down!

How about using FAITH, HOPE, AND CHARITY as your brain's default settings?

SOME THINGS WE CAN CHANGE,
SOME WE CAN EASILY MANAGE,
AND SOME WE COPE WITH.
THREE OUT OF THREE AIN'T BAD!

(Self-Awareness + Choice + Positive Conditioning + Reinforcement) x
Repetition
= POSITIVE CHANGE

I studied the whole flier, inhaling the bewitching scent of her patchouli. "But are you certain?" I asked her.

"There are no certainties, only possibilities," she explained.

"Isn't that particular statement stated as a certainty?" I observed.

"It's possible," she agreed, and was gone.

CLICK!
The CLICK of awareness.
The CLICK of forgiveness.
The CLICK of instant transformation.
The CLICK of recognition.
The CLICK of magic.
The CLICK of truth.
The CLICK of things falling into place.

CLICK.

CLICK.

CLICK!

TEN TIME AND LIFE MANAGEMENT TOOLS

Improving your time/life management skills is a piece of cake, but you have to really want to eat the cake!

1. **The To-Do List is a Must.** This is the easiest way I know of to accomplish more in less time. Simply write down the activities and tasks that you want to work on. Daily or weekly. Check them off when you complete them. "List the work, and work the list!" When you're serious about getting things done, the to-do list is your constant companion, friend, and ally! Don't use the list as an instrument of self-torture! You are master of the list, not the other way around. These are reminders—not "if you don't do *everything* on your list, you lose!" I also like adding a column for feelings/emotions I want to experience—the "to-feel" list, and a column for beliefs and values that I want to remember—a "to-believe" list.

2. **Know Your W.I.I.F.M.** "What's in it for me?" Why do I need or want to get more done in less time? Why DO I want to manage my life better? What are the benefits to me, my team, family, friends, community ...? Make a WIIFM list. Read your list every day for self-motivation, passion-amplification and memory-refreshment.

3. **Set, Revise, and Review Medium and Long-Term Goals.** The goals on *this* list are for the future—from a month to many years into the future. Help yourself make choices that are consistent with your "big picture" objectives. The more passionate we are about the goals, the better. No strong desire? Weak commitment? Look for the blockage, examine the evidence, review the WIIFMs. Bad goal? Change it! The magic is in the daily attention to your lists. The daily reminder is the key.

4. **Recognize and Defeat the Opponent.** Who or what are the demons that nick your enthusiasm? Procrastination?

Pessimism? Perfectionism? Paranoia? Pizza? Identify the opponent, and be the victor! For example, is procrastination your opponent? Then, notice your procrastination, read books about procrastination, visualize yourself overcoming procrastination, write a procrastination journal, recite anti-procrastination affirmations. Need I mention ... daily? Oh, and *don't wait!*

5. **Manage Your Stress by Choosing Gratitude.** Or choose to be neutral. Or choose to be philosophical. Just choose something and know that you are choosing it. Forgiveness is usually a practical choice. So is a humorous interpretation of events. Some like to use the "don't sweat the small stuff" reminder. Or... don't take yourself so seriously! The big idea is to become more responsive and less reactive, or in other words: more aware, conscious, in control and therefore, more efficient! Choose your interpretation. *Life is less stressful* when we make better choices. And sometimes we *can* choose between stress and peace. Not always ... but sometimes.

6. **Don't Invent Trouble When Trouble Doesn't Exist.** Isn't it a thrill to realize that some of our problems are self-created? Isn't it great when we stop! So, ask yourself: Am I making it up? And, if so, *why?* Unconscious habit? Do I have counter-productive interpretations or beliefs that need changing? Why would I choose to make myself irritable? Can I stop?

7. **Upgrade.** Would a better computer make your work go faster? Do you deserve a little more RAM? Upgrade tools and equipment, upgrade environment, upgrade confidence, upgrade attitudes, habits, etc. Sometimes even a small upgrade can make a huge difference in your productivity, and your happiness. Clear out some clutter.

8. **Reward Yourself.** A small reward in the middle of a heavy work day could certainly have positive impact. Don't use donuts, by the way, if donuts put you to sleep, or if you're going to feel guilty about it for the rest of the day. And be smart with your shopping—don't create *more* stress by rewarding yourself with something that puts you into debt. Even a cost-effective, one-minute gratitude break, mini-vacation visualization exercise, or quick walk outside can improve your mood *and* your work

output. The clear self-promise of a large reward (material, emotional, spiritual) for a large project well done might be the motivator you need to move it forward.

9. **Treat Every Friend, Family Member, Service Provider, Customer, Client, Vendor, and Coworker with Kindness, Compassion, and Empathy.** Even the difficult ones. This will potentially save you *years* of time.

10. **Read This Chapter Once A Week.**

BIG AND DIRTY LIES

1. If you have too much fun, the cops will arrest you.
2. If you make a funny face, it will stick like that.
3. Positive thinking is simplistic, and you are a jerk for believing it.
4. If our society agrees something is true, then it is.
5. The past causes the present.
6. If you have religion, you can take a nap in this lifetime.
7. Sex without love has no psychological effect.
8. You can't fight City Hall.
9. Happiness and joy are only for idiots.
10. It is impossible to have fun working.

POSI-QUIZ

1. When can I make the changes I want?
2. When can I succeed?
3. When can I contact the spiritual world?
4. When can I feel loved?
5. When can I heal?
6. When can I stop that pesky habit?
7. When can I improve my life?
8. When can I grow up?
9. When can I be real?
10. When can life be real?
11. When can I be happy?
12. When can I do that thing I always wanted to?

Answer key:
1. Now. 2. Now. 3. Now. 4. Now. 5. NOW. 6. NOW.
7. NOW. 8. Now. 9. NOW. 10. Now. 11. NOW. 12. NOW.

SO, HOW'S IT GOING, MIRACLE-MAKER?

"I don't care what you do for a living. If you love it, you are a success."
George Burns

"I still believe in love, peace ... I still believe in positive thinking."
John Lennon, in the film, *Imagine*

My guess is that you've participated in creating a few *awesome* miracles, and you're on the cusp of a few more! I'm also guessing that you might be ready for another goal clarification process, to help you focus and assist you in moving your life up a notch—to the notch of your choice.

Typically, ritual goal awareness days, like New Years Eve, birthdays, important anniversaries, remind us to make resolutions or changes or improvements, often in the form of a "lose-weight-stop-smoking-reduce-stress-stop-doing-something-bad-for-me" kind of goal. Other goals might be business (get more gigs) or financial (make more money). Accomplishment goals (write the book, make the recording) or healing goals (heal the rotator cuff, heal childhood emotions). Often, the achievement of one goal automatically brings with it the achievement of others!

And sometimes, we'll set a goal, or make a resolution—achieve it, and get a feel for the deep and profound effect it has, not just for our own lives, but for the lives of the thousands and thousands we're connected to, as well. We might consider it a turning point, or fork in the road ... an example of the butterfly effect, "sliding doors," fate, kismet, really good luck. Or, just call it a miracle!

Now, read each statement and jot down a few thoughts ...

"What really makes me happy?" _____

_____

"How can I do more of those things that make me happy?" _____

_____

"How can I bring more happiness to others, too?" _____

_____

People who collect guitars, stamps, antiques, memorabilia, often circulate want-lists to their suppliers and colleagues. What's on *your* want list ?

Material/Financial Stuff and Things Want-List: _____

_____

_____

_____

Emotions/Feelings Want-List: _____

_____

_____

_____

Wellness, Health and Healings Want-List:_____

_____

_____

_____

Spiritual/Metaphysical Want-List: _____

_____

_____

_____

Pick one of your most important goals/resolutions. Write it down here:

Now, imagine you have achieved success with this goal. What would be some of the benefits to you, your relationships, your health, your business? How does this goal make your life better? What are some of the positive payoffs? Please list six benefits that you reap:

1._____
2._____
3._____
4._____
5._____
6._____

A few more questions to ask yourself: Why do I want these things? Is this from the level of the rational adult, or the needy adolescent, or (yikes!) the helpless baby? Are these wants up-to-date, or ancient? When my goal is achieved, what will the impact be to me, my friends, my family, my community, my planet? Who or what determines what I want? Genetics? Sociocultural conditioning? Life's experiences making brain patterns? Parental training? Television? Billboards? Radio ads? Karma? All of these? Some of these? *None* of them?

Would you like a few more suggestions?

33 SUGGESTED POSITIVE RESOLUTIONS FOR THIS YEAR

This year I resolve—well, actually, I *vow*—to:

1. take total responsibility for my choices, decisions and moods.
2. return all phone calls promptly.
3. openly appreciate my friends and colleagues more.
4. seek healing for my hurts and enlightenment for my ignorance.
5. understand my own needs and recognize the wisdom of providing for them.
6. find the fun in my work.
7. be kinder to strangers, friends, family and co-workers.
8. visualize my positive future every day.
9. liberally practice forgiveness.
10. liberally practice optimism.
11. ask questions when I'm in doubt.
12. organize my goals and create a realistic action plan to achieve them.
13. keep a daily journal of my feelings, hopes, wishes and dreams.
14. be more aware of my impact.
15. honor my body as a temple and avoid poisoning it (too much).
16. be tactfully honest with others and bluntly honest with myself.
17. consciously create positive experiences.
18. transcend all limitations, especially the imaginary ones.
19. spend more time being nice and less time being grumpy.
20. see the positive possibilities in each and every situation.
21. be true to my deeply held values.
22. better manage my tasks, time, space and beliefs.
23. procrastinate no longer.
24. motivate myself to achieve what I really, really, really want.

25. create miracles, notice miracles and be grateful for them.
26. seek real solutions to my problems.
27. raise my personal standards.
28. laugh more and make others laugh more.
29. stop being petty.
30. do and say things that raise my confidence and enhance my self-esteem.
31. overcome my fear of success, fame and fortune.
32. break my negative addictions to self-pity, helplessness, perfectionism, etc.
33. cut back on worrying and begin practicing my faith.

And here are some more!

20 SUGGESTED POSITIVE RESOLUTIONS FOR YET ANOTHER YEAR

Taking responsibility for creating (or at the very least, influencing) my future,

I resolve to:

1. consider my mission in life before I speak or act.
2. discover my own "first aid" for pessimism -- and use it!
3. observe my habits.
4. keep my daily gratitude journal because it works wonders for me.
5. write down my brilliant insights so I remember and act on them.
6. win the war on pettiness, perfectionism and cynicism.
7. choose my dramas ... before my dramas choose me.
8. revisit and review books that inspired me the most.
9. signal before I make a turn.
10. judge ideas ... not people.
11. overtip.
12. tell at least one person a day, "I love you and I'm glad you're here."
13. ask for help.
14. accept help.
15. stretch my body, mind, beliefs and abilities.
16. respect copyrights.
17. find the sheer pleasure in my work, thus transforming it.
18. know how and when to depersonalize and stop playing the blame game.
19. respond to adversity by saying, "a positive outcome is possible!"
20. read and reread my resolutions every day!

Okay, one more set!

JERRY'S POSITIVE RESOLUTIONS FOR STILL ONE MORE YEAR

Pick your favorites and say: This year, I resolve to...

1. live my life as though everything is a miracle.
2. notice life-changing coincidences and amazing synchronicities.
3. express unconditional kindness as often as I want to.
4. practice moderation at all-you-can-eat buffets.
5. make my choices based on the outcomes I most desire.
6. tell myself three positive truths, for every one esteem-diminishing fib.
7. be early!
8. forgive much, especially when forgiveness is challenging.
9. manage my stress before my stress manages me.
10. take another heroic romp outside of my comfort zone.
11. confuse people less: increase honesty, decrease mixed messages.
12. learn something from every investment of money, time, love and trust.
13. return all phone calls in a timely manner.
14. find more opportunities to show appreciation.
15. make every day, a day of Thanksgiving (turkey dinner optional).
16. gracefully accept good advice when it is offered.
17. manifest creativity, passion and a sense of wonder in all things.
18. honor my ancestors; remembering, because of them... I was born!
19. be more generous with my service, resources and wisdom.
20. steal the BEST ideas and make them my own.
21. know and respect applicable copyright laws.
22. impact the entire universe with one small compassionate act.
23. spend less time surfing the net and more time creating my future!

POSI-YOGA: THE PRACTICE OF POSITIVE LIVING

First you "make believe" ... then you *do* believe. Let's say you want to be a recording artist, a music star. Start by writing your name in the Schwann catalog, and mocking up an album cover. Get some music magazines and glue your picture to the cover.

Want to sell some houses? Make up some little "Sold By Me" signs and paste them to newspaper listings and pictures of real estate. Make an endless loop cassette that repeats, "I see opportunities to make money everywhere!"

Maybe you just want complete spiritual and cosmic enlightenment. Make believe you see auras. Act as if the Supreme Being loves your style!

Metaphysically, you are CREATING YOUR REALITY with your visualizations, thoughts and feelings.

Psychologically, you are PROGRAMMING YOURSELF to take the right action to achieve success and remove your own blockages.

Give your God/Goddess *and* your subconscious mind a clear message of what you really, *really* want!

ANOTHER CUTE POSI-YOGA TIP

Sit in front of a piano or other musical instrument. If you've never played it before, that's okay! Imagine you are respected as a master of avant-garde performance on your instrument. Using traditional and non-traditional "playing," *express your current feelings*. There are no rules except: be honest with your feelings.

YOUR DAILY HOROSCOPE

This is a day to celebrate your life! I'm not kidding. Do it.

THE PATIENCE OF THE POSITIVE PATHWORKER

What are the talents, skills and habits you strengthened this year? How did you strengthen them? What positive outcomes resulted from your improvements?

As I type these words, I realize that my typing ability, for example, has really improved this year. I was mostly a hunt-and-peck guy, and now there are times that I don't even look at the keyboard! And my typing speed has significantly increased.

This "miracle of typing improvement" can easily be explained: success comes with more practice. The more you type, the better you become!

And, if we want to, we can also consider that my current high performance is the result of a set of causes in a historical timeline...

... from my first encounter with the typewriter (probably as an infant), my first typewriter (an Underwood from the 1950s), typing class in junior high (Hi, Miss Sasken!), to the term papers, first electric typewriter, business letters, the computer revolution, laptop keyboards, writing scripts, designing program material—you know, the whole history of "typewriters, typing, and me" resulted in this moment of "Now, I am an adequate typist!"

But wait! In order for all of *that* to have happened, my parents had to have met, and had to like each other, at least enough, to have me! And, if *any* of the gazillions upon gazillions of variables that let up to that crucial meeting of George and Irene, was different—just one little old variable *different*—I would not be here now, nor would you. I wouldn't exist, and you'd be reading something else, entirely!

And so it is, back and back and back, thousands of millions of years, gazillions times gazillions little variables, and here I am, typing these words for you now. And I'm not even looking at the keyboard (too much).

My ukulele playing has also improved enormously! Why? Maybe it was: practice, desire, imagination

karma, fate, synchronicity, motivation
natural ability, style match, the right location
quantum physics, reincarnation and solid motivation
having good instruments, and ukulele information
positive cogitation and a daily meditation!

WAYS I MADE MY DREAMS OF THE PAST COME TRUE

Stubbornly. Purposefully. Made them a priority.
Never gave up on them.
Didn't freak out too much.
Continually visualized the outcomes. Rode the ups and downs.
Stayed focused.
Made choices. Remained optimistic.

WAYS TO MAKE YOUR CURRENT DREAMS COME TRUE

Stubbornly. Purposefully. Make them a priority.
Never give up on them.
Don't freak out too much.
Continually visualize the outcomes. Ride the ups and downs.
Stay focused.
Make choices. Remain optimistic.

IMPROVEMENT TAKES PRACTICE.
Practice Promotes Improvement!

Practice the thoughts that create the successful outcome.
Practice the behavior that promotes the successful outcome.
Say the words that reinforce the successful outcome.
Feel the feelings associated with the successful outcome.
Yada, yada, yada ... abracadabra ... poof! Successful outcome!

POSITIVE BUZZ
Radio :30—Spot #1

Every kind act creates positive buzz.
Teaching creates positive buzz.
Sharing creates positive buzz.
Heartfelt prayer creates positive buzz.

Doing great work creates positive buzz.
Helping a stranger creates positive buzz.
Sincere smiles create positive buzz.
The right choice of words creates positive buzz.

Remember to generate positive buzz!

Think better words ... experience a better universe!

POSITIVE BUZZ—It's free! It's now! It beats the alternative!

A SHORT AWARENESS EXERCISE

When you watch *Seinfeld*, at any given moment, are you aware of a trained, professional actor named "Jason Alexander" playing (pretending to be) a fictional character called "George," or are you simply laughing at the antics of a person named George?

Try quickly switching from "Jason Alexander" awareness to "George" awareness, and back again.

At the restaurant, at any given moment, are you aware of a trained, professional service provider named "Betty" playing (pretending to be) an in-context, culture-appropriate character called "waitress," or are you simply ordering your food from, and (hopefully) giving a good tip to, the waitress?

Try quickly switching from "Betty the person" awareness to "the waitress" awareness, and back again. Does flipping "reality channels" activate and exercise new and interesting context interpretations, resulting in more options and opportunities, or is it just fun to do?

More importantly, are there some "reality channels" that are more useful than others? More joyful than others? More compassionate and loving than others? Kinder and smarter than others? If so, can we choose them at will? And if we can choose them at will, then why the heck don't we!

May we learn the impact of our thoughts, words and deeds ... and choose the best "reality channels" for optimal results!

YOUR DAILY HOROSCOPE

This is a day of transition. Relax! You'll get there.

YOUR CORPORATION

"Keep away from people who try to belittle your ambitions. Small people always do that, but the really great make you feel that you too, can become great."
Mark Twain

"Everything should be made as simple as possible, but not simpler."
Albert Einstein

I'd wager that you already have a pretty good idea of what to think, feel, believe, and do to get yourself from where you are right now, to where you'd like to be in the future—materially, mentally, emotionally, and spiritually. I'll bet that you also have some clear ideas about what that optimal future of yours could contain.

You are, in fact, the CEO of the corporation known as YOU and, as CEO, you pretty much call the shots. Your corporation has many divisions:

Financial Management
Mood Management
Communications
Asset Allocations
Human Resources
Research and Development
Division of Spirituality and Metaphysics
Scheduling
Health Maintenance

As CEO, you own quite a bit of stock (and stock options) in your corporation. Who else owns stock in YOU? Who has invested in you? Who cares about your success?

Mom and Dad?

God/Goddess?
Spouse? Siblings? Offspring? Family?
Friends? Allies? Coworkers? Creditors?

So, how much responsibility do we have to our shareholders and investors? Upon how many people does our success have an impact? Lots, I'd say!

Do you have a mission statement for your corporation? My mission statement describes my purpose in my life and my work—my reason for being. By reading my mission statement every day, I can remind myself what is important to me and remind myself to stay on track. It is my standard for my behavior and choices—a summary of my own priorities. My "magnetic North." My alignment tool. Guidelines for decisions. When I'm confused or overwhelmed, I can always read my mission statement. Here's the mission statement I wrote way back in 1996:

> I am committed to optimism, positive mental/emotional attitude and personal responsibility as my purpose and my cause—to live it, to practice it, to teach, inspire, and promote it. I am committed to finding and creating win-win situations for myself and every client that hires me. I am committed to making sure that my speeches, lectures, workshops, and seminars are practical by design, meaningful in content, and entertaining in presentation. Rather than promoting a quick fix; I stress the need for perseverance, practice and patience to break self-limiting habits of thinking, believing and behaving — while forming proactive, positive attitudes and beliefs, setting and achieving meaningful goals in the workplace and in life.

> I am committed to helping people elevate their self-esteem, improve their self-image and become more willing and able to make constructive choices and decisions. To these ends I continually strive to practice what I teach, to personally test and research the most promising, efficient self-improvement methods and motivational modalities available. I am committed to teaching realistic, results-oriented, practical tools and techniques.

My goals are simple: to make a positive difference in the lives of the people I teach and a positive contribution to the businesses that hire me. My mission is to do this with humor, love, compassion, humility, respect, and positive expectancy. I am dedicated to the truth that anyone can improve his or her life, work, and relationships by learning new, improved ways of thinking and believing—resulting in conscious, positive choices and decisions.

Your Mission Statement does not have to be as verbose as mine—it can be as short or long as you'd like. Ideally, it should be written so when you read it, you'll be inspired and energized. It can describe your work, your career, your personal life, or a combination.

Take a little time to work on one of your own. You won't be sorry!

YOUR DAILY HOROSCOPE

Notice what you're worrying about today. Stop worrying.

POWER TACTICS FOR POSITIVE CHANGE, PART ONE

"All change is a miracle to contemplate;
but it is a miracle which is taking place every instant."
  Henry David Thoreau

"You must change in order to survive."
  Pearl Bailey

"All life is an experiment. The more experiments you make the better."
  Ralph Waldo Emerson

"Sometimes its risky *not* to take a risk."
  Harvey MacKay

Of course, Thoreau was right. The miracle of change *is* taking place every instant. In nature. In technology. The job market. The economy. Fashion. The arts. In the orbits of the planets and the dance of our galaxy. Change is the name of the game ... of life!

We have already changed emotionally, physically, mentally, and spiritually from a baby, to a toddler, to an adolescent, to a young adult, to a mature adult.

Is the miracle of change unfolding in your life the way you'd prefer? Or do you expend lots of energy (unconsciously, of course) to avoid and postpone the changes you say you'd like? Change often requires leaving your comfort zone!

There are so many systems and teachings on the market today that offer information to assist us in our process of positive change—whether we want to break bad habits and form good ones, become smarter, more aware, more in control, more spiritual, more enlightened, make more money, or have better relationships.

Knowledge is power, but the practice and application of Power Tactics For Positive Change is much more effective than just reading about them. Why not design a personalized program of change with tactics that you will like, and that will be compatible with your lifestyle? *Why not?*

A strong desire for improvement, knowledge of your motivations, and commitment are prerequisites. It takes a strong purpose, a mission if you will, to bring you back on track when you get distracted by the million-and-one things that vie for your attention.

It is time now for your own experiment in positive change. Since the expectations of the scientist affect the outcome of the experiment (we humans do have biases, cultural conditioning and selective perception) let's choose to expect positive results.

Power Tactic 1:
Specifically identify the change you desire the most.
This is always the first step. The goal. The objective. The destination.

THE CHANGE I WANT THE MOST:

I want to change _____

_____

_____

to _____

_____

_____

Power Tactic 2:
Know your motivations—your reasons—for the change.

SEVEN GOOD REASONS WHY I WANT THIS CHANGE:

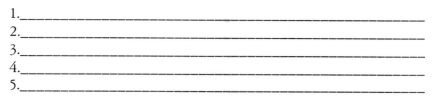

1._____
2._____
3._____
4._____
5._____

6._____

7._____

Power Tactic 3:
Question yourself about your change. Answer honestly.

Do my thoughts, beliefs, perspectives, interpretations and assessments of life support this change, or not?

Do I desire, imagine and expect that I can successfully make the change—or do my subconscious habits, patterns and expectations support the opposite?

Can I imagine myself in the future with this change? What does it look like? What does it feel like? How does it affect my relationships, my stress level, my lifestyle?

Am I willing to work for this change? How important is it to me?

Do I deserve to accept this change into my life?

Do I take the responsibility for creating and allowing this change into my life?

Am I willing to be patient with myself, respect and honor my own cycles?

Now, either "change your change" ... or proceed!

Power Tactic 4:
Experience your life as one continual process of change.

We have changed drastically since childhood. We've changed many things in the last twenty years, ten years, five years... maybe even the last five minutes.

A message that assists this process is: My life is all about change. I have changed in the past and I can change now. Change is not only possible—it is inevitable. And now, as a smart, aware, enlightened adult, I can consciously choose many of the changes I want. Change is my ally. A few things in my life that I have changed include:_____

_____

_____

Power Tactic 5:

Write down the change you want. Write it on a file card as a positive statement (a positive affirmation). Read it out loud at least ten times a day. _____

_____

_____

Power Tactic 6:

Become aware of role models for your successful change.

A role model is someone (real or possibly fictional) who is doing or has done what you want to be doing—and/or has the qualities you admire and want to embody. A role model can inspire us to believe in the possibilities for ourselves. A role model can provide valuable clues for us. How did *they* do it? A role model contains patterns of the change you desire—parts of your Future Self.

People who have achieved or embody the change I want for myself:

_____

_____

_____

I can have a "board of advisors." Five people, living or not, sitting around the kitchen table (in my imagination—my Inner World) giving me advice and encouragement. are: _____

_____

_____

_____

_____

Power Tactic 7:

Ask for help, and accept help.

Some changes require assistance. You might need advice and support from friends and family. Maybe your business network could help. If you are religious, pray for help! Need information? Google.com can help! Ask and accept. Ask and accept. Repeat.

Power Tactic 8:

Communicate to yourself that it is time for the change.

Use words in your conversations and thoughts that promote change. Change your routine and do a few things differently—especially the things that will promote your willingness to change.

For example: if you always have your radio or <Begin excerpting here> on in the background, try turning them off, and use the silence to think about your change. Rearrange your furniture. Get some new clothes. Buy new underwear. Break habits. Change the sequence of your usual way of doing things.

When you look at a clock or your watch, say, "It's time for change!"

Power Tactic 9:

Choose To Be Optimistic About Your Change.

Optimism seems to be the intelligent and empowering choice. Optimism triggers creative energy, and so does pessimism. <Begin excerpting here> both "work" to create, or influence, a result. Optimism can certainly catalyze miracles. Pessimism can also catalyze miracles, but in reverse! So, when you do catch yourself being negative about the change you've decided to make, recognize and identify that pessimist within. Who is it? Where does it have its origin?

Negativity, Fear, Doubts	Possible Origin
1. _____	_____
2. _____	_____
3. _____	_____
4. _____	_____
5. _____	_____

Do you really want to let this stuff influence you and your outcomes?

THE COMPLAINERS' QUARTERLY

Published by: You Never Do Anything Right, Inc.

Guilt's Cove, NJ

$ Too Expensive—Not Worth It ... Dissatisfaction Guaranteed

In this issue:

Kvetching for Fun and Profit!

The Many Ways to Expand Your Self-Pity!

Sabotage Your Holiday Season ... Here's How!

SPECIAL OFFERS

Tapes to Help You Screw Up Your Life

Professionally recorded and produced by the *Complainers' Quarterly* staff of negative thinkers, these tapes are real time savers. Listen while overextending yourself, or breaking commitments! Play them in the background while destroying relationships, suppressing your feelings, and fooling yourself! These tapes will intensify your depressions and misery, or your money cheerlessly refunded!

Instant Guilt

Poverty, Poverty, Poverty

Self-Pity Intensive

My Anger Prison

The Pit of Judgment—How to Fall In

Fear Unlimited

The Pity-Potty Training

New Dimensions in Passive Aggression

Addictions I Know and Love

"I See a Worm in Every Apple" and other negative affirmations by A. Growly

All of my problems are here to stay.
I can always see the misery in anything.
Everything bad always happens to me.
I am a jerk—past, present and future.
Nobody likes me, everybody hates me, I'm gonna eat some worms.
I am too complicated to be understood.
Nobody knows the trouble I've seen.
Every time I take a risk, I get burned.
All my relationships end in pain.

From The Complainers' Bookshelf:

Bashing the Child Within
Women Who Talk Too Much ... and the Men Who Hate Them
Be Your Own Worst Enemy
Don't Think ... and Grow Poor
Unlimited Powerlessness
The Name of the Game is Blame

Special Cassette of Selected Beatle Songs! Including:
I'm Down.
Misery.
I'm So Tired.
I'll Cry Instead.
You Never Give Me Your Money.
I'm a Loser.
No Reply.
Nowhere Man ... and much, much less!

Personal Ads

WM, 45, seeks illusion. Treat me as if you love me, then dump me. Cult involvement a plus! Box 82

Accident-prone WJF, 39, seeks male car dealer with good inventory. Would consider insurance agent or nurse. Anger repression turns me on! Box 73

Is your life a disaster? Mine, too! This bankrupt guy, 34, looking for ladies who appreciate dishonesty and charm. Let's delude each other! Box 66

Saint Jude ... where the hell are you?

YOUR DAILY HOROSCOPE

You will weather the storm.

POWER TACTICS FOR POSITIVE CHANGE, PART TWO

Power Tactic 10:

Process and heal emotional hurts from the past.

Intend to understand how hurts from the past are having an impact on your emotional present. Consider training yourself to become more aware of what goes on when you get angry or sad "for no reason." Look for the clues hiding in the past or in your biochemistry. Be the observer. Be the reporter. Be slow to judge!

Are you still thinking irrational thoughts and doing irrational things that are causing you pain? Well, stop that!

Writing in a journal can provide vital emotional feedback. Whenever you feel bad, sad, powerless, discouraged, angry, etc., write about it. Write about how you feel and what you think. Free associate. Write about anything you want to—no editing or self-censoring—this is private. Then read what you've written later on. You'll gain insight.

Become aware of where you give away your power. What or whom are you afraid of? Why? Are you turning the boss into Mommy or Daddy? Do you think some people better than you—and then resent them for it? Is this a pattern? Is it getting kind of old?

Become more aware of your "automatic-pilot" decisions, activities, relationships, and reactions that make you angry, humiliated, frustrated. Then, don't choose them! Notice habitual behaviors and beliefs (from the past) that you don't approve of now. *Consciously* choose positive beliefs, positive relationships, positive impact—a positive life!

If you need professional assistance with your healing, please get it.

Power Tactic 11:

Heal your Inner Child.

After getting into a relaxed, meditative state, imagine (visualize) you are having a conversation with yourself as a young child. Find out what he or she needs, wants, feels, thinks. In your imagination, give the child whatever he or she wants. We do have an unlimited expense account in our imagination! Explain things to them from your adult perspective. Love them. Nurture them. Help them. Treat them the way you would have wanted to be treated. Give her a pony. Give him a rocket ship. Give them messages of security, safety. Assure them that they are wanted and cared about. Tell them about your positive changes. Make contact with that Inner Child—the child part of you—every day!

Power Tactic 12:
Heal your Inner Adolescent.

Ditto for the part of you that is 12, 13, 14 years old. Give him or her messages of personal freedom, power, individuality, importance, confidence, ambition. Help her understand that everything she does or says *has impact* and she is responsible for their impact. Ask him to consider the possibility that he doesn't know everything, even though he thinks he does!

Tell your Inner Adolescent that people make mistakes and can be forgiven. Be a really good role model. Tell her not to worry ... she will grow up!

Power Tactic 13:
Heal your Inner Young Adult.

What were your hopes, wishes and dreams at age 17, 18, 19, 20? Remember them in meditation. Rekindle your idealism and belief that just about anything is possible. Ask for help from your Inner Young Adult to make your dreams come true. Deal with false status issues. Tell him that he will be learning so much more when he becomes older. Form a partnership with your Inner Young Adult. Create win-win situations. Be a mentor.

Power Tactic 14:
Name your best sub-personality ... and *be* it.

We are many personalities and identities. Find the one that has the most love, wisdom, power, insight, talent, confidence, creative ability, intelligence, intuition, spark-of-life, charisma, etcetera, and name him or her. It can be a nickname, a secret name, a code name, a real name. Identify with *that* one.

The most wonderful, powerful part of me is named:_____

_____

Power Tactic 15:
Write your personal mission statement and read it every day.

As you read in the chapter called Your Corporation, your personal mission statement describes and summarizes your purpose in life—your reason for being. By reading your mission statement every day, you remind yourself what is important to you, and to stay on track. Your mission statement contains goals and personal values. What is important to you. Some say it should be short enough to memorize. Others say the longer the better. For some, the personal mission statement is also their career or corporate mission statement. When confused or overwhelmed, you can always return to your mission statement.

What is the test of a good mission statement? It excites and motivates you. You get chills and feel excitement, you feel proud and purposeful. It is really *you*!

Power Tactic 16:
Write your eulogy and read it every day.

This is *really* long-term goal setting and a real short summary of your mission, and your essence.

What would you like to be remembered for? _____

_____

_____

_____

_____

Power Tactic 17:
Eliminate the word "try" from your speech and thoughts.

Yoda was right. When we "try" we might not "do." Telling yourself you will *do,* instead of *try to do,* just might give you the psychological/neurological/physiological advantage!

Power Tactic 18:
Stop fooling yourself!

Times of change are excellent times to look back in your history and remember when and where—and *how*—you fooled yourself. We all have a blind spot somewhere. By recognizing and owning up to our own patterns of self-deception, we can avoid them now and in the future.

When, where, and how I have fooled myself in the past:

_____

_____

_____

_____

Power Tactic 19:

Compose and use positive affirmations—words for positive focus.

Positive affirmations. Self-talk. Brain programs. Self-programming. Auto-suggestion. Whatever you call them, positive affirmations are empowering statements that support the changes you want to make. They are written in the present tense to describe the future you want to craft.

Usually, they are *part* of your program, not your *whole* program. On one level, affirmations *remind* us, on another level, affirmations *program* us—they adjust our selective perception. Affirmations keep us focused on making those positive changes.

Here are some examples of affirmations for positive change:

I am desiring, imagining and expecting my positive changes.
I am allowed to change for the better.
I have permission to change for the better.
Every day in every way I am creating positive changes.
Positive changes come easily and effortlessly to me.
I love the changes I am creating in my life.
I am guided by my highest intelligence.
I am determined to make positive changes in my life.
I am healing my hurts from the past.
I make choices and decisions that make me feel great.
I am responsible for creating my positive changes.

I am healing my Inner Child.
I am healing my Inner Adolescent.
I am healing my Inner Young Adult.

I am free to be creative.

I feel strength, security and enthusiasm in my choices.

I keep the positive power flowing.

I improve with age.

I appreciate every moment ... including this one!

My life improves daily.

I acquire valuable information and intelligence.

I give thanks.

I am gratitude in action.

I am love in action.

I keep a higher perspective.

I am fun and creativity in action.

I improve my ability to manage my nervous system.

I face the future with a smile!

I am always learning.

My grateful feelings are a constant in my life.

I consciously co-create my optimal future.

I am miracle-prone!

DO IT YOURSELF AFFIRMATIONS

Simply fill in the blanks. Or, use our suggestions.

I am changing my _____ (life, beliefs, underwear, habits, style) for the better!

Every day in every way, I am _____ (becoming cuter and cuter, learning more and more, getting better and better).

I am responsible for _____ (my every word and deed, my headaches, the national debt, my successes and failures).

I can beat _____ (depression, my addictions, my rugs, the competition, my own drum).

Yes, we do see things through many different sets of eyes:

the child "me"
the adolescent "me"
the adult "me"
the spiritual adept "me"
the angry "me"
the moody "me"
the happy "me"

So, which of my "parts" is doing the viewing? Which sub-personality is doing the judging? Each set of eyes sees the same event through different filters. Different experiences = different perspectives.

Affirmation
I am aware of which "part" of me is doing the seeing. I am able to change perspectives at will.

SHOPPING FOR UNIVERSES

If we aren't aware of choosing our universe, then our habits and patterns choose our universe for us. For example:

Universe #1: I'm healthy, wealthy and wise.

Universe #2: I'm totally psychic and can read auras.

Universe #3: I'm an idiot and I can't so anything right. I fail at everything.

Universe #4: I am really from outer space, and I'm headed home.

Universe #5: Whatever my mind can believe, I can achieve.

Universe #6: I am so in tune with my own Higher Power that I am in a constant state of bliss and ecstasy.

Universe #7: I'm a regular guy. I work. I go home. I watch TV. I go to sleep. I wake up again. I'm normal.

Universe #8: I create my own reality out of my beliefs, thoughts and feelings. I can discard most anything I really dislike.

YOUR DAILY HOROSCOPE

Today, you will be motivated to treat people with a little more tenderness than usual. Do it.

POWER TACTICS FOR POSITIVE CHANGE, PART THREE

Power Tactic 20:
Record your most important positive affirmations on a CD or cassette, and play them continually.

Reinforcement. Subconscious programming. The more you hear them, the more you'll think about them. Write them, record them and update them from time to time. Keep them possible and believable. Play them while you drive. Play them in the background when you're reading, working, cooking, etcetera.

Power Tactic 21:
Write your affirmations on file cards, signs, and sticky notes.

Motivational environmental art! Reinforcement, reminders and subconscious programming. Keep them simple and direct. Put them in your car, on your refrigerator, on bulletin boards, picture frames, your computer monitor, near the pet food, the microwave, the telephone, the TV, etc. When you see them, think about them. And smile!

Power Tactic 22:
Make The Commitment. Sign A Contract.
For example:

Contract With Myself

I, _____

am willing to commit

to spending a minimum of _____ minutes
each and every day to do whatever I need to do
to promote and create the following change in my life:

_____

_____

_____

Signed and dated,

_____

Power Tactic 23:
Develop an intimate relationship with your optimal Future Self.

Your Future Self is you in the future. There are many possible futures. Remind yourself of the elements of your preferred futures, and make your choices based on the outcomes you most desire.

My *preferred* future feelings: _____

_____

_____

My *preferred* future career/work: _____

_____

_____

My *preferred* future relationships: _____

_____

_____

My *preferred* future abundance: _____

_____

_____

My *preferred* future values: _____

_____

_____

Power Tactic 24:
Use your favorite spiritual/metaphysical techniques ... DAILY.

Practice your faith. Pray. Meditate. Chant. Talk to your Higher Self.

"Re-examine all you have been told in school or church or in any book, and dismiss whatever insults your soul."

Walt Whitman, Leaves of Grass

Power Tactic 25:

Discuss your positive change with the right people, not with the wrong people!

Sometimes the alchemy of change is delicate. Other people's energies and attitudes could impact your outcomes. Sometimes you need to network with hundreds of people, and sometimes you need to be discreet. Avoid sharing your miracle-work with jealous, negative, critical folks. *Do* share your process with supportive allies and loved ones. Know the difference.

Power Tactic 26:

Be on the lookout for information and inspiration for your change.

You never know where or when the key to your positive change will appear to you. Watch TV with a pad and pen, jotting down ideas and information. Carry a small tape recorder or digital recording device to capture your great ideas and cosmic revelations. Keep a pair of scissors with you when you read the newspaper and magazines. Create a file. Make a scrapbook.

Power Tactic 27:

Visualize/imagine what your positive change looks and feels like.

The power of creative imagery/visualization/imagination is used in every self-help, self-improvement, self-healing, personal growth system I've ever studied. Athletes, performers, salespeople, business people, musicians, healers—they all do it. Daily.

Power Tactic 28:

Eat well, sleep enough and exercise your body.

Wrong foods = less energy! Not enough sleep = less energy! Not enough exercise = less energy! Certain vitamins and nutrients might be helpful. Be sensitive to your physiological needs.

Power Tactic 29:
Manage your tasks better.

Write and review your to-do list every day. Be sure to include your positive change on your list. Prioritize.

Power Tactic 30:
Invent your own POWER TACTIC.

Power Tactic 31:
Do your work –– and let go!

Don't worry or fret. Have hope and faith. Anxiety is the dream killer.

Power Tactic 32:
PRACTICE, PRACTICE, PRACTICE, HAVE PATIENCE!

"All glory comes from daring to begin."
Eugene F. Ware

"Nothing is more likely to help a person overcome or endure troubles than the consciousness of having a task in life."
Victor Frankl

Power Tactic 33:
Create and use your own, custom *Positive Change Program*.

Your program is the application of the Power Tactics that you really like, that you will really use regularly, that will work for you. Your plan must be practical, realistic and have a little fun to it! Of course, the more motivated you are, the more time and effort you'll put into your plan.

Here's an example:

My Custom-Designed Positive Change Program

The change I want to create is: I want to be more successful at my work.

194

This is my program:

— Write positive affirmations, put them on cards where I can see them every day:

"I am improving my performance at work"

"I am finding ways to enjoy my work more"

"I am becoming more successful at my job"

— Once a month, visit the library and take out a book with info that will help me. Take notes as I read. At least one book a month.

— 10-20 minutes of daily meditation, visualizing myself being more successful at my work.

— Make daily and weekly to-do lists. Keep one schedule in one place.

— Get a little digital recorder, carry it with me *always*, record my insights and suggestions to myself.

— At least every other day, do an Inner Child meditation for 10–20 minutes.

Is it possible that this book is the last "self-help" book you'll ever need?

INFORMATION... WILL... LOVE

"As a general rule, the most successful people in life are those who have the best information."
  Benjamin Disraeli

"The difference between a successful person and others is not lack of strength, not lack of knowledge, but rather in a lack of will."
  Vince Lombardi

"Love is all you need."
  John Lennon, Paul McCartney

No matter what I do, no matter what I think,
I am still my father's son.
I have the raw materials to work with.
Transcendence can be fun!

Appreciate the light bulbs of knowledge, glowing.
Appreciate the friends we continue knowing.
Appreciate the ancestors that cleared the Path for you.
Appreciate the love you know is true.
Appreciate disappointments that teach you great lessons.
Appreciate fine restaurants and funky delicatessens.
Appreciate the wisdom you seek and seek and seek.
Appreciate the challenges you've met this week.
Appreciate the brilliantly designed machines.
Appreciate the great books and cool magazines.
Appreciate the ones who gave you your start.
Appreciate the miracle that still beats your heart.

Health issues come and go.
Business can be fast or slow.
The stock market goes up and down.
Some moments you smile, some moments you frown.

Babies are born while others pass on,
Some deals are terrific, some are a con,
And *you* decide how to make sense of it all.
You buy stuff online, or go to the mall.

Pray for peace, and choose to be sane,
Hope for the best, and hope for less pain,
Do your best and strive for better,
Accept love, know love, and write a love letter!

Learn the meaning of *your* life ...
Easing the suffering, reducing the strife ...
Applying your skills, with maximum goodwill ...
All in all, existence is a thrill!

Can you remember how you pray (or hope, or wish) when you're desperate? That intensity and focus! The emotional involvement! The authentic experience! Why not pray (or hope, or wish) in that style *all* the time?

Do you think the intensity and emotional focus somehow amplify the power of the prayer (or hope, or wish)? Or, does it make your nervous system more likely to imagine, believe, and in the end, *create* or *manifest* the desired result in the physical world?

Does focused desire, or intention, somehow juggle subatomic particles, which in turn, juggle atoms, and then molecules, and cells, and ... and ... and ... Or, is it going with the flow that creates the best "luck"?

Life on Earth does seems fraught with contradictions. We don't particularly need to add to them. So choose your mission and purpose. Make your choices based on the outcomes you most desire. Always take the next step on the Path. One step at a time. One right after the other.

Let's not ignore or waste the precious gifts we're given daily!
Precious gifts.
Daily.

THE DEDICATION

"Give me a lever and a place to stand, and I will move the world."
Archimedes

"A friend, I am told, is worth more than pure gold."
Popeye the Sailorman

If you were writing a book, who would be mentioned in your dedication? Who are the people who helped you on your way? Who loved you, assisted you, nurtured you, encouraged you? Who inspired you, saved your life, told you the truth, taught you? Who coached you, gave you a break, understood you, cared about you, had faith in you? Who totally changed the course of your life ... that resulted in this incredible moment of Now?

Certainly, we owe our lives to the ones who came before us—Mom and Dad, grandparents, great-grandparents, great-great grandparents, and all the way back! Without them... no us!

As we grew up, we had neighbors, relatives, buddies, favorite TV and radio personalities, recording artists, authors... We had many school teachers, guidance counselors, advisors, coaches, music and art instructors, mentors... We had relationships of all kinds: dating, romances, marriages, offspring ... roommates, colleagues, bosses, coworkers, clients, customers, vendors, business owners, service providers, politicians... We had heroes, role models, people who catalyzed great changes in us through love, through adversity, through pain, and through pleasure!

Is it possible that the ones we disliked the most—the ones who were the biggest pains-in-the-butt, the ones who were *so* difficult—what if they were the ones who made some of the greatest contributions to our growth and development? Is it possible? Is it time to forgive them, and maybe even, *appreciate* them?

Spend some time today thinking about the people who love you, and who loved you a long time ago. While you're at it, think about the people who have helped to change your life. What do you remember about these people? What did you learn from them? What did you learn from knowing them? Does your list overlap? Where are they now? Thank the ones you can find. Tell them what they did for you.

THE HERO

Someone real who inspires you to positive action.

Provides guidance for YOUR choice making and reality creation.

Demonstrates qualities of the future-self you wish to become.

Fill in the blanks.

My childhood heroes were _____
_____

because _____
_____

My adolescent heroes were _____
_____

because _____
_____

My current heroes are _____
_____

because _____
_____

GETTING A GRIP

"We have to try to cure our faults by attention and not by will."

Simone Weil

Here's a fun way to diffuse anger, without breaking furniture. When intense anger has entered your being, excuse yourself and go to a bathroom that has a mirror. If a bathroom isn't available, a car's rear view mirror, a pocket mirror, or the mirror on the ceiling of your bedroom will do. It is preferred, however, to do this anger-removal magic in private. Here's what you do:

1. Look at yourself in the mirror for one minute, and breathe.
2. Make the most angry faces you can for the next minute—the more grotesque, the better.
3. For the third minute, make the funniest faces you can. Stick your tongue out, roll your eyes, make funny noises if you wish. Make believe you are having fun.
4. For the fourth minute, simply look at yourself in the mirror, and breathe. Take deep breaths and relax.
5. Say to yourself, "I am now choosing to release my feelings of anger. I still might not like (the cause of the anger), but I don't have to stay bent out of shape over it!"
6. Feel good that you did something wise and powerful. Enjoy that good feeling.

If you must be angry at someone, why not get angry at the parts of yourself that sabotage your own happiness? Then, speak to those parts, identify their ages, understand their anger, give some love to those parts... and see what happens!

Friends and spouses help you see your stuff, and *force* you to deal with it. Friends and loved ones provide an easy way for us to see ourselves. They trigger personal growth. They piss you off. They love you. They show you your "good" and "bad" parts. They are mirrors.

MORE MIRACLES

Each and every day, and that includes today, contains at least one:

- huge blessing.
- obvious challenge.
- very important lesson.
- wonderful gift.
- cool opportunity to strut your stuff.
- awareness of an authentic miracle in your life.
- miracle decision ...
- miracle choice ...
- miracle response.

Right?

Right! Look for them. Daily! Remember the *miracles.*

Okay then. Supposing today's important "life lessons" (the experiences that make your stomach feel funny and shift you into an altered state of consciousness) were unconsciously custom-created *by* you *for* you, and for some specific reason? What if we interpret the consequences of these lessons as "life's tuition fees?"

What if our primary occupation really is Student Of Life? Is it possible that we are old enough to understand the game of life, to know when to take things in our stride, when to cry, and when to laugh? When to let it go? Is it time to connect with your Higher Purpose and proceed with greater joy than usual?

Isn't it great to really get it, to really understand someone's problem-making behavior—a client, a friend, a business associate, a boss, a guest—when their hurt and defensiveness is translated into anger and rudeness right at you. And yes, you did have a part in creating the proceedings but still, you've decided to perform an act of "by the book" service recovery, unconditional kindness, perhaps, taking the high road, being the adult person in the equation, and feeling quite good about it?

Is it possible that our priorities are in need of a review and some reorganizing? Do we sometimes forget what our lives mean? Need a little reminder? I'd write a list (or write in my journal) if I were you. It really helps!

So then, what are your current priorities? What is your life all about? What's in the mix, and in what proportions?

Consider what these words and phrases mean to you:
- money
- family
- friends
- doing good works
- having emotional mastery
- your service to others
- sex
- food
- material goods
- a walk in the woods
- Seinfeld
- mind meld
- Lenny Bruce
- the squirrel and the moose
- American Idol
- Midol
- The Gospel Singer
- Corporal Klinger
- Debra Winger
- John Coltrane
- that trip to Maine

Consider my list and jot down your own.

YOUR FINAL DAILY HOROSCOPE

Today is the day that demonstrates that this stuff *works*!"

ABOUT THE AUTHOR

For more information about Jerry Posner, and about his lectures and seminars, please visit www.jerryposner.com, or write to posgroup@aol.com.

415710

Made in the USA